Charles Welles

Three years' wanderings of a Connecticut yankee

In South America, Africa, Australia and California. With descriptions of the several countries, manners, customs and conditions of the people. Vol. 1

Charles Welles

Three years' wanderings of a Connecticut yankee
In South America, Africa, Australia and California. With descriptions of the several countries, manners, customs and conditions of the people. Vol. 1

ISBN/EAN: 9783337196783

Printed in Europe, USA, Canada, Australia, Japan

Cover: Foto ©Andreas Hilbeck / pixelio.de

More available books at **www.hansebooks.com**

THREE YEARS' WANDERINGS

OF

A CONNECTICUT YANKEE,

IN

South America, Africa, Australia, and California,

WITH

DESCRIPTIONS OF THE SEVERAL COUNTRIES, MANNERS, CUSTOMS
AND CONDITIONS OF THE PEOPLE, INCLUDING
MINERS, NATIVES, ETC.

ALSO, A DETAILED ACCOUNT OF

A VOYAGE AROUND THE WORLD,

ATTENDED WITH UNUSUAL SUFFERING, HARDSHIP, PRIVATION, DISAPPOINTMENT,
AND DANGERS ARISING FROM FEARFUL STORMS; THREATENED WRECKS
ON ROCKY COASTS, AND AMID REEFS; BY FIRE,
DECEPTION, MUTINY, ETC.

ALSO, VARIOUS INCIDENTS OF LIFE ON SHIPBOARD.

By C. M. WELLES.

Illustrated with Beautiful Steel Plate Engravings.

SOLD BY AGENTS ONLY.

NEW YORK:
AMERICAN SUBSCRIPTION PUBLISHING HOUSE.
1860.

PREFACE.

Love of adventure, ambitious schemes, romantic enterprises, and visionary projects of some sort, seem preëminently the characteristics of men of the nineteenth century — especially of young men.

Gold has become the absorbing object, and thousands have sacrificed all that was dearest and best — made shipwreck of all that was purest and holiest — in their attempts to realize these golden dreams. Although, in a majority of instances, the sequel has proved the fallacy of these ambitious hopes and designs, they still are slow to believe the testimony of those who have tried them, and many are still rushing to remotest shores for anticipated gain.

The present volume is but one of the "*beacon lights*" on this broad highway, thronged by the over-confident and ; if it persuade any of these of the superiority of well-directed energy and ambition, if it serve to awaken in any more just conceptions of the true and worthy ends of life, if it create more enlarged and liberal views of the claims of the world upon individual men, the efforts of the writer will not have been in vain; these chapters of living, actual experience, of stern reality, will not have been wrought out to no purpose — for whoso is instrumental in adding a new link to the chain of improvement, does something in the great and good work of encircling the world with beauty and gladness; and that this effort may do some small service in this direction is the humble hope of the author.

C. M. WELLES.

CONTENTS.

CHAPTER I.

Adventurous Aspirations of Early Youth. — Desire to see the World. — Visit to New York. — Ship for Australia in the Bark Peytona. — Deception in procuring a Ticket. — Disorder among Officers and Crew. — Impressions of Life on Shipboard. 9

CHAPTER II.

Seasickness. — Mistaken Ideas of a Voyage. — Alarming Indications of the Ship filling with Water. — The Green Mountain Boy. — Attempt to throw the Captain overboard. — Beauty and Majesty of the Ocean. — French Celebration. . 26

CHAPTER III.

Ill Forebodings. — Treachery of the Captain. — A Sabbath-Day Picture. — Cornish Miners. — Code of Laws. — Government of the Ship. — Disturbance, and its Causes. — Discipline, &c. 44

CHAPTER IV.

Personification of Neptune. — Discovery of a Barrel of Apples. — Efforts to obtain Water from a distant Ship. — Joy on seeing Land. — Appearance of the Natives on the South American Coast. — Manner of Life. — " Catamarans." . 66

CHAPTER V.

Landing at Bahia. — Beauty of the Tropical Scenery. — Visit of the Custom-House Officer. — Trouble by Reason of an undue List of Passengers. — Description of the City. — The Climate, Soil, and Buildings of the Place. — Visit into the Country. — English Chapel. — Market Places. . . . 85

CHAPTER VI.

Romance of a Walk in the Tropical Region. — Indications of former Splendor. — Effort in proceeding on the Voyage. — Difficulties in leaving Port. — General History of Brazil. — Death from Delirium Tremens. — Narrow Escape from Fire. 109

CHAPTER VII.

Burial at Sea. — A Lunar Bow. — Table Mountain. — Terrific Storm. — Landing at Cape Town. — Rambles about the City. — Imprisonment of the Captain. — Visit to Seyola, the Kaffir Chief. — Prayer Meeting on Ship. 134

CHAPTER VIII.

Byron's Sea Enthusiasm. — Make the Harbor of Port Louis. — Visit the Isle of France. — Delightful Scenery. — Grave of Harriet Newell. — A Malabar Funeral. — Embark in the Brig Nautilus. — Revolting Fare. — Land at Melbourne. . 160

CHAPTER IX.

Stay at Canvas-town. — Journey to Ballerat. — Purchase of a Claim. — Location of Tent. — Housekeeping. — Experience in the Mines — Disappointment of the Wardy-allock Expedition. — Return to Ballerat. 179

CHAPTER X.

Various Adventures in and about Ballerat. — A Magpie. — Visit to Creswick Creek. — Power of Kindness over Convicts. — The Old Woman. — Walking Leaves. — Take the Sacusa for Callao. — Description of Australia. . . . 200

CHAPTER XI.

Monotony of Sea Life. — Change of Time by the Omission of a Day. — Landing at South America. — Disappointed Hopes with Reference to Gold. — False Reports purposely circulated. — Stay at Lima. — Earthquake of 1746. — Roman Festival. 223

CHAPTER XII.

Pleasure of "Variety." — Proximity of Joy and Sorrow. — The Yellow Fever. — Voyage to Panama. — Arrival at San Francisco. — Scenes at the Post Office. — Situation of the City. — Impressions of Different Men. 251

CHAPTER XIII.

Life at Sacramento City. — French Creek. — Captain Pike. — "Sly Diggings." — Mud and Diamond Springs. — School Houses. — Mammoth Trees. — Snakes. — Mountain Scenery. — Influence of Curiosity. 273

CHAPTER XIV.

Mormon Refugees. — Visit to Gold Canon. — Varied and rough Experience among the Mountains. — Return alone to Sacramento. — Night in the Cave of the Hermit. — Solitude. — Its Effects. — Lonely Camping in the Woods. — Digging at French Creek. 296

CHAPTER XV.

Residence at San Francisco. — "Pop-Corn Institution." — Life on Steamer Cortes. — Pearl Islands. — Interview with Father Guernsey. — Missionary Tour. — School Teaching. — Camp Meeting. — Their Influence in New Settlements.   . 319

CHAPTER XVI.

Voyage Home. — Attempt at Suicide. — Natural Features of California. — Its beautiful Climate, fertile Soil, and delightful Scenery. — Reflections upon Men and Manners. — Superiority of American Character and Genius.   343

THREE YEARS' WANDERINGS.

CHAPTER I.

ADVENTUROUS ASPIRATIONS OF EARLY YOUTH. — VISIT TO NEW YORK. — SHIP FOR AUSTRALIA IN THE BARK PEYTONA. — IMPRESSIONS OF LIFE ON SHIPBOARD.

WAS there ever a boy who did not *expect* to travel and see the world for himself? The early and prominent characteristic of enthusiastic boyhood is a love of novelty and adventure; and when this is fed by the glowing descriptions and stirring details of interested travelers, wonder and curiosity cannot be restrained, and the desire to *see* and *know* becomes an almost irresistible impulse. Ignorant of the " enchantment " that " distance " sometimes " lends to view," other lands and climes seem like the " Elysian fields " of classic fame. The broad ocean, with its rolling tides and sweeping billows, bearing on its crested bosom proud ships, with their snowy sails; the great beauty of natural scenery in certain localities; odorous gales from island shores; golden treasures imbedded in the richly freighted earth,— all come home like so many notes of bewitching melody, kindling the fervor of youthful imagination, to make the world appear a perfect *El Dorado* of hope.

Wiser people may descant upon tame realities that dissipate the charm of actual experience, and on the folly of aimlessly pursuing the phantom; but the reply is usually like that of the aspiring youth to his father, offering like counsel under different circumstances—"I would see the folly for *myself*."

Such, emphatically, were my own feelings. A desire to see the world had haunted me for many years, by night and by day, and was continually prompting me to the formation of some plan by which my fond anticipations might be realized.

Receding months and years, however, seem destined to bear nothing to me but the unsatisfactory experience of *deferred hope*; for, in truth, I was no favorite of Fortune, and the "unconquerable bar of Poverty" ever mocked my progress, though it in no wise tended to diminish the ardor of my adventurous spirit. In the month of December, 1852, while out of business, I visited New York, still on the alert for every indication that betokened the dawning of that era, the attractive features of which, I confidently hoped, would fill the records of my future history with well-acquired glory for myself, beside imparting somewhat of pleasure and benefit to others.

Little did I think, upon my first landing in the city, the first link was already formed in the chain of circumstances that was conspiring to bring about the long-desired result.

Repairing to the docks one day, my mind, as usual, filled with visionary schemes, and in my heart half envying those already upon the surging waves, who were so much nearer the goal of their ambition than I, my attention was arrested by a handbill with the most inviting caption: "YACHT EXCURSION TO AUSTRALIA."

The Peytona, it appeared, a clipper bark of the first class, six hundred tuns burden, would leave the port, on the approaching first of January, for Port Philip and Melbourne.

The fair representations were seized with avidity, and I longed to enter at once a career of such prospective brilliancy.

Flattering inducements were held out to those who were desirous of making the voyage, as the notice will show.

"*She will be fitted up in a style as elegant as unique, and fresh provisions will be furnished for nearly half the voyage. It is confidently expected she will land her passengers at Melbourne on the sixtieth day from New York, including stoppages. No such opportunity as this has ever been offered to gentlemen desirous of visiting that enchanting region. It is not fair to compare this ship with the ordinary class of vessels hitherto fitted out, and now advertised for Australia, as the Peytona is above competition from any quarter. She will take an experienced surgeon; and all the attention of a first-class hotel will be granted in the most liberal manner.*

Proprietor,   CAPTAIN A. PELLETIER,
98 *Wall Street.*"

A rare opportunity indeed! was my mental soliloquy. Who knows but the favorable time has come for me? I desire to go; and this, perhaps, may be the key that will throw wide the hitherto barred gates of the world for my entrance. I *will* enter "a first class hotel," too. Cleopatra's barge would sink into insignificance beside our floating palace, and all her *et ceteras* be as nothing in comparison with the luxurious surroundings that would be ours in the two months' journeying to the "enchanted regions." A second thought, however, served to weaken the foundation on which my airy castle had been so suddenly reared; for the sober conviction forced itself upon my mind, that a penniless, friendless youth, like myself, was in no promising condition for such an enterprise.

Notwithstanding this, I was firm in my determination to go, if possible, and if difficulties would obstruct the open path, they should but incite to greater action, and perchance they might vanish, in the beginning, before the energy of a resolute will.

I at once conceived the importance of preliminary measures, and to this end repaired to the office of the proprietor, where I had an interview, the result of which was, the promise of a free passage to Australia, provided I could insure six passengers for the Peytona, beside myself.

Now, I verily thought, the "cloud" was pierced, and its "*silver lining*" fully displayed, so bright and strong were my expectations of promised pleasure. Stories of the rich profusion of shining ore in the land whither we were bound, were already in circulation, and I doubted not it would be an easy matter to enlist the requisite number for the accomplishment of my purpose; being aware that men in general consider no prospect more alluring than the easy acquisition of golden dust.

My mind, of course, naturally reverted to my Connecticut associates as the surest source from whence I could draw the little company; and, intent upon the feasibility of the project, I hastened home, and with earnestness becoming a good cause, endeavored to infuse into the spirit of others some measure of that enthusiasm which animated my own.

I found my coveted reward in a sufficient number of pledges to enable me to look forward with confidence to the fulfilment of my hopes.

It is not necessary for me to recount the incidents; the feelings that influenced, and the motives that actuated, our little band in the speedy adoption of the plan. Nor is it essential that I specify the reason which induced me to apply nearly all my own scanty funds for the purchase of a ticket for my young fellow-townsman and friend,— John Harman,— one whom I regarded as even more unfortunate than myself.

Beside us were Harry Yates, Jim Darrow, Buckley, Smith, and Brown; seven " poor but virtuous" men, ill-used by fortune, and little careful whither fate should lead them.

For myself, the world opened before me a broad and inviting field of action, and my feet were burning to tread the farther shore of the vast ocean.

It took but a short space of time to complete our arrangements; and these at an end, we bade adieu to the familiar scenes of

Hartford, and if we felt an emotion of regret at the last look of her receding spires, they were mostly stilled by the powerful voice of Hope, which beckoned us away. On the 25th of January of the new year, we all met on board the Peytona, lying at the dock, foot of Wall Street; it having lingered thus far beyond its appointed day of sailing.

We selected our berths; placed our names respectively on each; arranged our chests in front as seats, and were ready, as we bravely thought, for any and all events.

Still day succeeded day, without any signs of departure, until the 29th, when orders were issued for passengers to pay their fare and secure tickets. I collected my friends in the office of the captain, introduced them as such, and saw them produce the requisite material for the purchase of a passport through.

I felt somewhat sensitive in seeming to have paid my passage, by securing theirs, and consequently remained silent till they left, when I asked the captain for my ticket, and was surprised to meet with a peremptory refusal. To this I remonstrated, but to no purpose. I could do nothing. I saw his advantage, and concluded there was no alternative for me but to give the contents of my slender purse into the hands of the miserable deceiver. I did so, and from the meager pittance remaining, I bought three cheap shirts, and a scanty steamboat blanket for my friend John, and the same for myself. This done, my earthly possessions consisted of a few clothes, a watch, and two dollars and a half in gold, wherewith to make the voyage to Australia.

Memory recalled the instance of a traveler who equipped himself satisfactorily for a voyage around the world with only a tin cup. Though I professed to believe, more or less strongly, in the doctrine that "man wants but little here below," I must confess to a decided reluctance in narrowing down the circle of my desires to actual necessities in my own case; much less to bring myself to the meritorious standard of my illustrious precedent.

Disappointment indeed lingered upon the very threshold of my course; but the decree had gone forth, and I chose not to revoke it.

The impression was unavoidable that something was wrong. The rumor was in circulation that some of the New York passengers had placed an injunction upon the vessel, and at this juncture of affairs, had money been plenty, or even employment in the city, my delegation from the Nutmeg State might have been strongly tempted to abandon the voyage. We wandered about, meeting daily to consider matters; sometimes on board the Peytona, sometimes on the Battery, and again at Pelletier's office. A constant watch was maintained, as something in the conduct of the captain intimated there might be an object to accomplish in sliding off without us.

On the 9th of February, however, we had the satisfaction of seeing the vessel start from her quiet moorings; and as this day marks the beginning of the records of this eventful period of my history, I shall transcribe incidents as they were penned at the time in the order of their dates.

We are now at sea; and such a prospect! no better than a floating bedlam, notwithstanding all the fair promises of order and comfort. This afternoon a steam tug made fast to us, and Pelletier, appearing among the men, ordered some of them to weigh anchor, no one, apparently, being appointed for the purpose. At the same time a proclamation was issued that the passage tickets were to be taken, and all those not determined to go must return.

The official command of the ship, it seems, is to be assumed by Jackson, whom Pelletier has introduced to the ship's company as captain — a tall, broad-shouldered, hard-featured, red-faced, grizzly-haired, brandy-looking old fellow, without a single redeeming quality in his unprepossessing exterior.

All assembled on deck to gaze at the pleasant scenery about the Bay, being somewhat elastic in spirits, in spite of depressing influences, and prepared to appreciate the motion of the bark after so long a time of inexplicable detention. The city and the shipping have been saluted with innumerable disorderly cheers, for the idea of doing things "decently and in order," in this Babel-like confusion, is out of the question.

We have a strong reënforcement of passengers from the steamer while passing down the

Bay, making *comfort* a word of still more doubtful meaning than before.

The tug has cast off, and a few men, with their hearts failing them at the eleventh hour, have returned with her.

Captain Jackson, duly installed in authority, stepped forward on the deck, singing out at random, "Forward, there! H'ist away that jib!" "Loose that fore-topsail, will ye?"

As no one responded to the call, it caused a look of astonishment, a moment's hesitation, and then in a voice that reminded me of a tornado, came the exclamation, "Where the — is my crew?"

A ridiculous query! it seemed at the moment, though, as it proved, not altogether unseasonable; for, upon inquiry, we find the officers, beside the captain, to be Payson, the first mate, a stalwart down-easter, and Grant, the second mate. Of course we are minus a foremast hand. A momentary lull in the hubbub and turmoil of multitudinous voices and movements followed the outbreak, but was suddenly disturbed by the loud ejaculation, "I'm one," from a hard-looking young fellow, who seemed almost the personification of recklessness. "Come, boys," he added, looking, apparently, to some of his comrades, and in a few moments a crew was enrolled from the list of passengers, to whom usual wages were promised. They immediately turned to, the orders were repeated, and in a little time sail was made upon the bark, and she was laying her course.

Confusion is not confined to the ship's crew. Unexpected perplexity arises also from other sources. As for us Connecticut men, however, we are snugly ensconced in our recess, dimly lighted with a "bull's eye" in the deck, and to be sure well-strown with trunks and chests.

Our number is diminished by one, he having received a letter from his wife almost at the last moment, full of pathetic appeal, which influenced him to relinquish his golden hopes, and return, no doubt thinking, with the poet, "Be it ever so humble, there's no place like home."

Into his place, and one other bunk of our compartment, we have admitted a very respectable Englishman and lady — Mr. and Mrs.

Hope; rather close packing for delicate, feminine natures, but under the circumstances she may consider it *good fortune*.

The Peytona has accommodations for only one hundred and fifty passengers, and we have, at least, two hundred; making fifty, who, in the nature of things, can have little opportunity to enjoy the benefit of "tired nature's sweet restorer," provided Morpheus should deign to visit such scenes of confusion at all. Of course Pelletier, in his grasping meanness, has sold the places twice over.

Among the last arrivals are some fine-appearing French people, who have reposed a misplaced confidence in their smart compatriot of Wall Street. We have also a German lord,— no less than the high-born "Prince Paul, of Wirtemberg,"—the well-known naturalist,— a portly and pompous personage, with a truly aristocratic gait, apparently not less than seventy years of age. The house on the quarter deck, it seems, he had engaged exclusively for himself, suite, and baggage, and had paid for the same in advance.

His effects were sent on board, and they

were thrown on deck by an indifferent person, where they remain hopelessly scattered, with a vast quantity in like predicament.

As for his prepaid quarters, he finds encamped therein a crew of regardless and unterrified New Yorkers, who laugh him, his princeship, his pre-payments, and his peremptory commands, to scorn. One little berth only, in the cabin, is allowed him; and as for his suite, nobody knows where they are.

We have had supper, — state-prison fare, — at least I can think of no hotel, (to quote our advertising promises,) except the public house at Sing-Sing, where "every attention" certainly means no more than it does here; a few pieces of boiled beef, served in tin pans, baker's bread, a tub of butter, and a barrel of apples. The grateful smell of the beef, while cooking, was rather cheering to our olfactories, and we made ready, though soon convinced that *conventional readiness* was entirely superfluous.

No table invited us to a quiet meal. Half a dozen men secured a beef pan, each for himself proceeding to operations with his jack-knife.

I made sure of my allowance by taking a slice from a loaf, seasoning it at the butter tub, pocketing an apple, seizing a modicum of beef, and retired to a corner.

"All the attention of a first-class hotel, boys!" shouted Yates, as I was escaping from the crowd. A loud laugh showed the appreciation of the hit at the false pledges of the owner.

It is quite late as I write, and the vessel is not still yet. The bunks are full, and the remainder of the unhappy passengers are laid out on the table, or promiscuously strewed about among the baggage.

We are a miserably cheated company; so much is evident already. I believe we present a more perfect spectacle of dire discomfort and confusion than was ever before witnessed, especially in such narrow limits. Some exceptions, however, in a group of men; English factory operatives, apparently, who seem determined to bring harmony into confusion, if they can not educe it *from* it.

They have traveled before, and have cunningly selected the best-lighted part of the "saloon," as we call the steerage, and there, seated together, they have remained during all the unutterable disturbance — the swearing, quarreling, searching for sleeping places and baggage, lamentations and reproaches; imperturbably scraping and blowing upon two fiddles, a clarionet, accordeon, and trombone, as peaceably as if they were on Parnassus, instead of a place well-nigh resembling Pandemonium. Their music possesses but few charms, except for their own enraptured selves, however.

No better opportunity, I imagine, to test character, in all its points, than life on shipboard. Every variety of disposition is here fully manifest; every conceivable phase of human nature openly developed; and whoever comes out of the scathing ordeal, " possessing the soul" in patience and integrity, may be set down as perfect heroes and heroines, fully prepared to act well their part in the great drama of life, whatever it may be, or wherever.

CHAPTER II.

SEASICKNESS. — MISTAKEN IDEAS OF A VOYAGE. — ALARMING INDICATIONS OF THE SHIP FILLING. — DISORDER AND MISMANAGEMENT AMONG THE CREW. — THE FRENCH CELEBRATION.

10th. — Great abundance of haggard faces this morning, indicating unrefreshing sleep, imperfect ablutions, and, if I mistake not, sincere and early repentance of this most unpromising adventure. A majority of the ship's company, including even Payson, the mate, have been seasick. I am constitutionally free from this tendency, consequently have had an opportunity to show forth practical sympathy in efforts to promote the comfort of the poor creatures lying about on deck in almost deadly misery, groaning most pitifully, and refunding their provisions.

The sea is rough, and the day has been showery; but the close air of the steerage is unendurable, and they must needs take the pelting of the rain, and the "chilly nor'-wester," with the slender and only consolation that recovery will make better.

Many and sorrowful are the wishes I have heard expressed from one and another, that they had not left home and home comforts, good situations, good business, kind friends, to suffer so much, merely for the chance of gain, by toiling for gold in a foreign land. My attempts to console them are seconded by one of the passengers, a tough old sea captain, who is constantly repeating the animating words, "Cheer up, my lads; never let your hearts fail you!"

There is, after all, considerable practical sense in the story of a father who had a son strongly desirous of a seafaring life, and his ingenious method of cooling his aspirations. He gave him a powerful emetic, shut him up in a box, intrusted it to a man, with instructions to jolt him about the streets for an hour or two. It is unnecessary to state the subject was never broached again.

People contemplating a sea voyage usually think so much more of the dangers to be encountered than of daily privations and disagreeables, that they neglect to provide many little articles indispensable to comfort and convenience on a long voyage.

This is eminently the case with our company. Very few are provided with more than an outfit for a short land journey.

They seemed to forget they could not practice shopping every morning, or perhaps imagined the ship would afford an inexhaustible supply.

To travel commodiously and pleasantly at sea requires more philosophy than to live on land; more apparatus and foresight than journeying on Terra Firma.

One or two speculative fellows, with an eye intent upon their own interest, having some understanding of the matter, have laid in generous supplies of certain miscellaneous commodities, such as soda-water, crackers, chocolate, confectionery, cigars, woolen hose, &c., which they readily dispose of at treble their cost.

11th. — Yates, who has been to California,

has suggested a division of the steerage company into three messes. The necessity of such an organization is too evident to allow objection, and they are at once enrolled, numbered accordingly, and to each a carver is voted, for the purpose of serving out the food in an equable manner — a most welcome change.

"Smouging," a contemptible name for contemptible stealing, has been the order of the day.

Yates apprised us in season of the universal imposition practiced upon ocean passengers by giving them tolerably good fare at first, and wretched afterwards. Judging, from our first day's experience, we could not presume upon imperial luxuries to come, and considering the necessities of the case, the facts stated in Harry's exposition, additional matters well known to us, such as the mysterious disappearance of the half-emptied butter tub at the very first meal, and like things, we deliberately agreed to "smouge."

"Good!" said Harry; "there's a barrel of first-rate bread now, and we shall have miserable stuff before two days are over. Let's fill our bags with that!" No sooner said than done. Half a bushel was secured in a dirty clothes bag, pillow-cases served for the rest, and the spoils were hung at the head of our bunks.

An arrangement entered into from sheer necessity, with an eye to the future, not ours only, but our companions in misery.

12th. — No appropriate sights or sounds usher in the peaceful hours of the sacred Sabbath. No service, neither place, preacher, nor congregation; and, indeed, almost any thing might be nurtured to worship as easily as this sick, unhappy, and restless crowd.

General low spirits have predisposed the passengers to fright. A few angry-looking clouds this morning gave rise to all sorts of prophecies of coming storms, and many doleful stories of shipwreck and peril.

A squall struck us suddenly, and threw us nearly on our beam-ends, and for a moment we thought to realize them. The alarm was instantaneous and great, for the ignorant majority thought their last hour had surely come.

Some one, more experienced, cried out jeeringly, "Put a handspike in the lee scuppers and right her," which only served to increase the discomfiture of those untutored in nautical expressions and affairs.

Suddenly the cry arose, that the ship was filling, and must inevitably sink. The captain himself seemed to believe it, and uttered various exclamations of fright, which alarmed all, especially the women. An examination was immediately held, which showed five feet of water in the hold, beside several inches on the cabin floor, surging about, wetting every thing and every body.

Nobody knew from whence it came, the ship having been considered uncommonly stanch and tight; but the discovery was at length made, that the ventilators which opened under the bulwarks, just above the deck, had been open since leaving port, and the heavy sea, beating against the sides of the ship, had forced the water through them. The ventilators are now closed, and strong bands of passengers are relieving each other at the pumps. All our "smouged" biscuit are ruined. They must go overboard to-morrow. Some truth in the proverb, "Stolen gear never prospers."

14th. — Sunday night the pumps were in operation the whole time, freeing the ship by morning, with no more harm done than the thorough drenching of baggage and stores, many of which seem to have been resolved into their original elements.

Yesterday the wind increased to a gale, the sea rose until it constantly swept us fore and aft, and poured a steady stream down our miserable hatchway. The water rose inch by inch about our feet in the cabin, which caused another fright, as many were not sure but it rushed in at some leak. Coverings were taken from the bunks and injected into the wide space between the hatchway, and the ill-fitted "umbrella," or outer cover; but one after another they washed through and were carried out to sea, till every one in the saloon was gone. During the excitement, the captain appeared, lantern in hand, pretending to search for the source of the water in the cabin.

He insisted upon all believing it came from

the hold. His superior wisdom and obstinacy, however, are mainly attributable to the influence of the intoxicating draught, which unfits him to navigate even himself correctly, much less a bark like this, freighted with human souls.

During the continuance of the gale, Fowler, a Green Mountain Boy, — a profane, careless fellow, — was exceedingly terrified by the unaccustomed sights and sounds of the storm, and threw himself upon his knees, crying vehemently for mercy, and that he might be restored safely to his native land.

The sailors, indignant at his unseasonable devotions, and still more at his being in their way, roughly pushed him aside; but the poor fellow withdrew into another place, to continue his supplications unmolested.

How instinctively the heart of man knows the true and only source of help! — *knows*, yet wilfully neglects it.

The over-crowded vessel had not afforded room for all the baggage, nor all the heavy freight; consequently a large number of trunks and packages had been lashed to the quarter-deck. This began to break loose, and Payson, the mate, ordered them to be thrown overboard.

Some of the passengers reluctantly commenced the work of destruction; but the captain soon countermanding the order of his first officer, they desisted.

Our bark was in violent motion, and freight, casks, baggage, and every thing else were precipitated from side to side with fearful rapidity, to the imminent peril of every life and limb on deck.

Absolutely it must go, order or no order, or the ship could not be worked; and again they resorted to the necessary expedient, only to meet with a second rebuff from the captain, who stood with "quarter-axe" in hand, threatening to cut down the man who persisted in such a course.

At this, half a dozen seamen sprang at him, and had he not been too much intoxicated, a serious affray might have followed. As it was, it proved but a brief struggle before he was disarmed, overpowered, and secured. The men in their rage threw him over the sides of the ship, and were on the point of giving him a cold bath, when some one, expostulating, caused him to be drawn in, when they thrust him into his state room, and turned the lock.

Soon after, while pacing up and down, and looking at his window, I was horrified to see his infuriated visage directly before me, and his pistol aimed at my head. "Click!" went the lock, and for an instant I thought myself a dead man. Fortunately the weapon missed fire; I speedily sought safer quarters, at the same time shouting to one of the crew, "Jim, he's got his pistols; he's got his pistols, and has just fired at me." "Never mind," rejoined he, coolly, "we drew the charges before we let him have them."

In a few hours he was liberated, and came out determined upon revenging such treatment; but the passengers assuring him all would be right in the morning, he retired, and this morning at daybreak appeared, apparently calm.

There has been no little excitement and dissatisfaction among passengers from the very moment of departure. It has become a fact well known among us, that two captains, successively engaged by Pelletier to command the Peytona, discovered upon inspecting the ship's papers, so much evidence of informality, and such an illegally large number of passengers, that they refused to command her.

Our provisions are scanty, and barbarously ill-served, beside being crowded almost beyond endurance. The ship's management has been so utterly loose and reckless, that even we, inexperienced landsmen, can not fail to see it.

A thrill of horror ran through us all, in addition to the tumultuous yet indefinable apprehensions that stirred every bosom upon the discovery that the ship and all it contains was in the charge of a miserable inebriate.

Suspicions are growing upon the mind of Buckley and Smith, the eldest of our special group, as well as myself, that there is a dangerous gang of men on board, from whom something is to be feared.

Among these are "Big George," the first who volunteered as seaman, those who responded so promptly to his invitation, and several others, including Maginnis, the carver of the second mess. The latter, we are confident, from every indication, has already had experience of the "Convict's Home."

All these are included in the "*Stowaways*"—those who hid themselves on board till tickets were collected, and the vessel under way.

Having thus secured free passages, they emerged from the coal-hole, or peak, an insufferable little den under the forecastle, and other secret places, mingling boldly and unquestioned with the rest of the passengers. It is said they came from Brooklyn, and have contrived this means of seeing the world at the expense of the ship, ready for the performance of any thing, however treacherous or cruel, which they may consider for their profit or pleasure. Payson, the mate, is evidently leagued with them.

Circumstances are not wanting to show that the attack upon the captain was designed for the mate's promotion; that his thorough-going partisans, having their own way, would have dropped him into the sea, in order that their chief might assume the command. What plans he and they may have, further than this, we can only conjecture.

It has become a matter of consultation with the passengers, whether they shall not insist upon making some port immediately, some suggesting Bermuda, and others a return to New York; for the prospect of performing a voyage of twelve thousand miles in safety, under the control of a tipsy commander, seems dubious. But there are many who prefer to go forward, and a change of destination could hardly be effected, having no leader or concert of action.

17th. — Yesterday the mate convoked the two cooks and stewards from the cabin and steerage, and recapitulated to them the numerous complaints against them for filth, negligence, and disorder, ending with abundance of threats that they should be elevated to a position altogether different from any they desired, unless they reformed in these particulars.

To-day the doctor, — not the ship's surgeon, but the cook, to whom the sailors had given the title of M. D., not having the fear of this admonition before his eyes, became intoxicated, and set the galley on fire.

With some there is much unpleasant feeling toward the supercargo, who has induced the captain to break the promise, made the morning after his imprisonment, not to drink any more, and there are those among the passengers who even threaten to throw them both overboard. So much endurance is hardly to be understood. Some captains would have placed men in irons for such conduct. Surely we are an undisciplined crowd.

Some of the Brooklyn gang have been playing a game upon our butcher, too. This official, a green Dutchman, who has but few qualifications for his present berth, had a pig to kill.

Sailors have but little reason to expect any thing more than salt beef and hard bread under any circumstances; and knowing if they could spoil his work, it would be their fun, and not their loss, they volunteered to take Hans under their tuition, which they did, instructing him to skin the pig, taking from it an enormous thickness of good meat, and leaving nothing but a mutilated skeleton.

There is no use complaining to the captain. One only meets with an indifferent reply, be the matter what it will, unless it be something that affects his fancied, personal dignity.

19th. — We have had three days of pleasant weather; have improved it in clearing the cabin, which was becoming extremely forbidding to any lover of neatness.

Clear skies and balmy air have indeed proved humanizing in their influence. Many of the passengers are earlier and more thorough in their ablutions, less inclined to discord, and the evenings are enlivened with music and conversation. There is something beautiful and majestic in the appearance of the broad ocean, sparkling in the clear light of the moon; something terrific and grand in its tempest-tossed billows, stirred to fury by an angry storm.

No divine service to-day. Alas! the captain does not allow it.

22d.— Monday morning the steward became

so much intoxicated we had no breakfast until ten o'clock. An indignation meeting was held by the passengers, which resulted in the dismissal of the delinquent official, and the election of Anson Carrington, an intelligent young fellow, to fill his place. More disturbance again to-day. Hearing a tumult above, I went on deck, where I found undue excitement between some of the French passengers and the chief mate, with one or two seamen. The sailors stood with knives drawn, and the impulsive Gauls were armed with bayonets obtained from a rack in the cabin.

The captain saw fit to interfere at this time, and with pistol in hand, succeeded in parting the combatants without bloodshed.

24th.— This day marks the anniversary of the exile of Louis Philippe, and the birth of the French Republic of 1848.

The Frenchmen have had a grand jubilee over it, commencing with a national salute at sunrise, from our two quarter-deck carronades, and followed by loud cheers at the elevation of the French flag, in no wise intimidated by the thoughts of its being contrary to law. In close conjunction to this, the "stars and stripes" of our own America were floating in the breeze, all unconscious of the incongruous portion of mankind it was waving over. A band, organized from the available material on board, played "Hail Columbia," and the "Marseilles Hymn."

To this succeeded a formal entertainment for the whole ship's company, the delicacies of which consisted of raisins, dried beef and herrings, almonds and soda crackers. This was enlivened by enthusiastic speeches, songs, and toasts, not altogether inappropriate for the commemoration of a French revolution, and concluded by no less enthusiastic fighting.

The mate, contrary to custom, as well as the steward, were intoxicated. The transition from angry words to blows was quick and sudden. The captain was strongly solicited to interpose, but, being in no condition himself for sober reflection, his only answer, prefaced with an oath, was, "Let them fight it out."

The matter, of necessity, was taken in hand by others, and the feeling subdued for a time;

A SHIP SPOKEN. 43

but the mate soon flew into a rage, seized whatever weapons were at hand, and hurled them at whoever came in his way. He was taken and closely confined, where a few hours served to quell the violence of his passions, and excite in him deep regret for his disgraceful display, after having so long been an advocate of peace, temperance, and good order.

We must have presented a somewhat curious aspect to passing vessels. At 10 o'clock, A. M., while in the midst of some patriotic demonstration, with flags flying, gunpowder burning, people shouting, we spoke ship Herculean, from New York to San Francisco. The captain hailed us, asked the usual questions, and was somewhat curious to know who we were, and what we could be doing. The ships kept close company for some hours; when, a moderate breeze springing up, we left them with nine hearty cheers.

If this be *patriotism*, O country! thou mightst well blush for thy sons.

CHAPTER III.

ILL FOREBODINGS. — TREACHERY OF THE CAPTAIN. — A SABBATH-DAY PICTURE. — SHIP GOVERNMENT. — DISTURBANCES. — DISCIPLINE, ETC.

"THE thing in the world I am most afraid of is Fear," said Montaigne, "and with good reason — that passion alone, in the trouble of it, exceeding all other accidents." Some appreciation of this sentiment was mine, as I sat down to record the events of the 27th.

Vague and growing apprehensions of some indefinable ill seem to agitate the minds of the passengers, not only as regards the ultimate success of the voyage, but our immediate safety.

Since the assault of last week it is evident that, either from jealousy or some other cause, an almost deadly hatred exists between the captain and mate. Additional evils are feared from such an alienation of feeling among the principal officers of the ship. Many are desirous of making the Cape Verde Islands, now about a thousand miles distant, that they may escape as soon as possible from this scene of drunkenness and confusion.

The supercargo, who has seemed of late to have considerable control of matters, and to be the only person worth applying to for redress, now appears to the passengers to be far from friendly.

He has had charge of the stores, and for some unknown reason has made way with or secreted the best of them, leaving for us nothing but hard bread and "salt junk," otherwise called "old horse," both being the cheap, ordinary fare of common sailors; and this, evidently, what remained of some previous voyage. However strong the desire may be for an early port, the captain will doubtless be deterred by the probability of being detained in any port we might enter, for irregular papers, on account of the number of passengers so far exceeding the legal proportions.

Yesterday, to the utter astonishment of all, we were placed upon short allowance of water, only three pints "per diem" being measured out to each person, for all purposes of cooking and for drinking.

This course, when only eighteen days out, excited great surprise, and instituted active inquiry. A mass-meeting was convened upon the quarter deck, and Carrington, our lately elected steward, placed in the chair. A committee of investigation was appointed — Smith and Buckley, and one or two from the first cabin. They proceeded at once to the exercise of their functions; searched the hold as far as possible, and returned in a half hour to report a scarcity of water, for even for one week, at the three-pint rate. It was hereupon resolved to petition the captain to put into the nearest port; all considerations of inconvenience yielding to the imminent necessity. The document was drawn up, signed, and duly presented to the captain by a deputation chosen for that purpose; but being stupefied with the "fiery element," he coolly received it, and laid it aside, with no answer whatever.

"Hope," to us, is where it was in the poet's vision — "*aloft.*"

March 1st. The vessel was headed for the much-wished-for port, a day or two after the petition; at least, so we were told by the commander; the reality of the thing we have no means of knowing. He refuses to acquaint us with our true position, working out all his observations alone, and turning a deaf ear to all inquiries made as to course or distance.

It is true, an occasional notice of latitude and longitude is posted on the bulletin, side of the quarter-deck house; but such is our confidence in the veracity of our captain, many of us think he would as soon make false entries as correct ones. We begin to be panic-stricken lest we die of thirst.

Our ears have been greeted by the information to-day, that we are past the latitude from which we could have made the islands, and consequently must resume our southward course.

A more thorough search below, however, has resulted in the discovery of three hundred gallons more of water — a circumstance that allays the fears of some, but only appears a temporary quiet to others, considering the length of the voyage.

After a new and solemn trial, we have a verdict to discharge the baker from his situation for fear of sinking the ship with his heavy bread.

5th, Sunday. Yesterday we had another cry that the ship was sinking—a state of things ascertained to have been brought about by the carelessness of the officers, who had neglected the occasional pumping, usually necessary at sea. A broil occurred between the captain, mate, and supercargo; but we have come to consider fighting one of the common occurrences of the day. We have excitement daily; more on the Sabbath, often, than at any other time; making the day one of unrest, rather than rest. A reflective spirit, for once, seems hovering over all, and what is more, there seems a yielding to the spell. It is afternoon, and we are sailing quietly, about five degrees north of the line, before a gentle breeze. A group of men stand leaning over the rail, gazing at the eddies under the stern; finding in the quiet of their own thoughts, for the time, a solitude as perfect as though in the midst of a desert. As for myself, I have secured a private apartment, by means of a borrowed blanket, and a coil of hawser lashed to the top of the quarter-deck house, and extended to the rigging by rope-yarns, &c. Agreeably to the "systematic disorder" of our condition there is no store room for the sailmakers, and our spare sails and cordage are all lashed upon this narrow roof. The largest coil on the after-starboard corner I have appropriated to my own use, and by a tacitly recognized law, this has become my sleeping place on pleasant nights, and my snug retreat by day.

Here I can sit and write at my ease, and at the same time take observations of those about me, if I wish.

Smith and Buckley are playing the agreeable to the ladies, Mrs. Hope and Egan, who are enthroned upon a couple of water casks, forward of the cook's department. A quiet company in the maintop excite strong suspicions that they are engaged in the unseasonable diversion of card playing. Forward, the watch are mending clothes, relating tales of no serious character, or asleep in the shade.

The movements of some dozen or fifteen persons, who have constituted a sort of " radius vector" around the mainmast, are somewhat amusing. The heat is such, we often sit all day in some shady place, fearing, if left, it would be lost.

To the shades of the mainmast, accordingly, this little band of patient creatures resorted after dinner; and as the sunshine gradually shifted from over the swelling mainsail, falling upon them, one and another would change their position, bringing about a slow motion, reminding one of the hour hand of a clock.

But, list! strains of music. Ah, it is " Home, sweet Home." How it sends a thrill through my heart, and moisture to my eyes! and there is no difficulty in discovering that others are affected in like manner.

We have been twenty-four days out; and in that time have become a little commonwealth by ourselves, with such marked individuality as to attract the attention of others.

The party of which I am a member are all, with the exception of Mr. and Mrs. Hope, from the "land of steady habits," and no disgrace,

I would fain believe, to our native state, though the praise must be understood as comparative, for the various thefts which we have executed, and are still executing, severally or together, although not less justifiable, perhaps, than the appropriation of the Indian corn repositories of the starving Pilgrims of Plymouth, two hundred years ago, yet would scarcely redound to our honor if performed while living at ease in good old Puritan Hartford, among the descendants of the Hookers and the Ellsworths.

We pass, however, as a very respectable and intelligent circle, and are counted such desirable associates, that we are continually solicited to receive one and another into our little brotherhood, but decline doing so, thinking it more prudent to maintain a polite yet firm exclusiveness.

One group attracting some attention is the music-loving Englishmen, already alluded to, whose astonishing choice of a time for instrumental performance was during the very first evening of sailing, when scarcely a semblance of organization was visible, and a note of harmony seemed impossible.

They have stuck together with a true John Bull-ish spirit, sneering at every thing, and constantly telling how much better things are managed on board "Henglish ships." They create some amusement by their ultra-Yankee opinions, and half vulgar slangs and solecisms, yet form no undesirable feature of our social evenings with their music, vocal and instrumental.

In the first cabin are quite a number of French passengers, some of whom seem persons of respectability and fortune, who appear, by a peculiar sort of interest in the voyage, to be in some way connected with Pelletier, the miserable owner, or the more dangerous captain.

The house on the quarter deck is still occupied by the New Yorkers, whose treatment of the old prince, Paul of Wirtemberg, has already been noticed. This gentleman seems to have lost many of his treasures at the time so much was consigned to the deep. Also, Mr. and Mrs. James, English people, have lost trunks containing goods estimated by themselves at twenty thousand dollars, which they were transporting to Australia for the purpose of establishing themselves in business.

The prince's suite, whether it was large or small, suddenly disappeared when he came on board, taking advantage, doubtless, of the double-refined, high-pressure style of republican independence which is the fashion among us.

He seems to have plenty of the exhilarating beverage, and by dispensing this liberally, he maintains a fair understanding with those he chooses to make his friends; but his unpleasant disposition and filthy personal habits make him an object of repulsion to very many.

These New Yorkers we imagine to be clerks and foremen — scheming fellows, but unsuccessful in money matters, and are therefore repairing to the golden regions to acquire the fortune their own land denies them.

Among the rest are a dozen Cornish miners, athletic men, who, with their mining tools and other accoutrements, constitute a mess by themselves, occupying the whole of the midship house.

They are extremely quiet, admit no one into their fellowship, show such a united front, and so much physical force, that nobody cares to annoy them.

Such are the component parts of our little nation. I speak of *republican* government; but it sometimes seems an anomalous compound of the despotic and the patriarchal, or more, perhaps, like the times when "there was no king in Israel," and every man did that which was right in his own eyes.

There is some discipline among the sailors, such as it is. The captain, when not too much intoxicated, stands boastingly on his own dignity, seemingly regarding the passengers as a herd of inferior beings. He vouchsafes no information as to place or prospect, except in extreme cases, ever replying that he is master, and if he knows where the ship is, and where she is going, "it's enough." All matters relating to those on board he leaves to their own unassisted management, with the exception of serving out food and water, which he and the supercargo seem to arrange together.

We have therefore gradually arrived at a sort of unwritten code or common law, which the common sense of the whole body upholds, and which is promptly sustained whenever necessary by individual might, mass meetings, &c.

Theft of things necessary and convenient is allowable, as in Sparta, so that our Bill of Rights, or fundamental laws, might be compendiously stated thus: —

1. Every man for himself.
2. Steal whatever you wish, if you can find it.
3. Act decently, unless it is out of the question.

As an example of administrative proceedings under the code, I cite the following instance: —

Two Italians, who occupied the same bunk in the forward part of the steerage, were observed never to undress. To say nothing of the influence on the olfactory organs, we knew such doings, persevered in, to be provocative of infectious disorders, and remonstrated with them quite strongly, but to no purpose.

Accordingly, some half dozen combined early one morning, and dragged them, in spite of their resistance, to the top-gallant forecastle, the appointed place for ablutions, where they were regaled with several buckets of clean sea-water, rather unceremoniously administered. With this encouragement they speedily indulged in a little wash, and a change of linen, such as they had.

With the liberty of the second article, one might witness our "smouging" a whole cask of porter, twelve dozen bottles, from the deck, first taking the superfluous precaution in our scrupulousness to ascertain that no one knew its owner.

We arranged the bottles snugly under the mattresses in our bunks, and drink the black tonic at our leisure. Mr. and Mrs. Hope share with us, of course, though it has proved a decided misfortune to the latter. Upon her feather bed, the pride and delight of her heart, one or two bottles have been unfortunately broken, saturating it in such a manner as to insure its complete ruin. Notwithstanding the joint opposition of its owners, it has been thrown overboard. The old lady has more than once been found in tears, well nigh proved to rise from this dreadful loss, while we, unfeeling creatures, are cruel enough to laugh at her calamity.

March 8th.—Lat. 5° north. Cool and light

winds. Captain proposes to steer for South America. Official jealousy and rum, however, are causes of almost daily trouble between the captain and his officers, preventing united action in any thing. Bloodshed was only stayed to-day by the interference of passengers.

9th. — Very hot and calm. Sea smooth and glassy. Nothing breaks the absolute motionless glitter of its surface, except a broad and gentle swell, silently and steadily approaching us from the north, scarcely disturbing our tranquillity, as it passes beneath and by us, in its course toward the south.

From my retreat in the hawser, I gaze upon the wide expanse, and a solemn awe steals over my mind, as I think of the glory, majesty, and power of Him " who holds the waters in the hollow of his hands," gives them their appointed bounds, controls the winds and the storm, and sends forth, at his will, his messengers of fury, or mandate of " *Peace.*"

I shall take advantage of the quiet in penning the history of a day's experience on board.

We rise when we choose. All who could find a place have slept on deck since coming into warm latitudes, so that there is even less ceremony than usual, most making nothing but a "dog's toilet," giving a jump and a shake, and it is done. As for myself and friends, we make it a point to take a thorough bath before breakfast, which we accomplish by successively throwing water upon each other. This we find to contribute much to our health and spirits, beside keeping us in gaining order, despite our hard fare and bad lodging.

Almost the first sound that greets our ears in early morn is from the "Doctor," who thrusts his frouzy head from his room, shouting, "First mess."

The steerage steward repeats the words, and soon a hundred different voices reëcho the welcome call, at which multitudes seize their pails, basins, plates, tubs, or whatever utensil they have, and rush for the place of attraction, knowing the proverb to be in full force, "First come, first served."

The hungry men arrange themselves in a line, not unlike those at the "General Delivery" of a Post Office, while the carver delivers to each his allotted portion.

While the earlier ones are served, the rest have time to jump up, secure their dishes, take their places behind, and in ten or fifteen minutes the mess is served, and a shout of, "Second mess," summons another group. All scatter about the vessel to eat, some in the rigging, some on the rail, and others on the water casks. Harman, Yates, and myself usually meet on the roof of the quarter-deck house, where, with conversation alternately jovial and serious, we dispatch our coarse viands, which are scarcely sufficient to meet the demands of our generous sea-appetites. The first cabin and officers are served with some pretense of form, while the sailors have last and least of all brought before them in a wooden tub. Tubs are also used for the Cornishmen, and the New Yorkers, who do their own dividing, but have little relish for their coarse style of food.

Indeed, all of us have many times quoted the fallacious promise of the advertisement. This morning, as Yates and myself each drew from one pocket his piece of hard beef, and from the other the still harder cracker, while sitting on the hawser, Yates held his up, one in each hand, saying, archly, "All the attention of a first-class hotel."

The New Yorkers seem unable to take things merrily, seldom making a joke of their condition, or, at least, only a sour one. They often hail the advent of their meal, especially if the wooden tub contains a good, hearty soup, with, "Here comes the swill."

Breakfast over, we have the time till dinner to mend and wash clothes, which latter process is accomplished by soaking them thoroughly and towing them overboard all day; in telling stories; reciting prose and poetry; reading to each other; playing at cards or chess; lounging about and sleeping, or doing nothing whatever. These occupations are varied by scandal, news, and other occurrences, corresponding to the excitement of newspaper paragraphs in land communities. Indeed, most of our scenes are as warlike as Othello's fortunes.

It is rumored that the steward's wife has been flirting quite unjustifiably with the mate; another version has it with the supercargo —

a circumstance which accounts for the constant quarreling between these domestic and nautical officials.

At one time a disturbance was noticed in the small, open space before the companion way, soon ascertained to be John Newman, one of our English steerage musicians, a bragging, gaseous son of Bull, scolding at Harman. A ring of pleased spectators gathered as quickly as to a "dog fight," and in like manner encouraged the disputers. From words they were on the point of coming to blows, when the burly face of the old captain was seen on deck, aiming at the company at the same time, a "nine-cornered oath," and two six-barreled pistols. Fear of the reckless commander quelled the tumult, and the crowd, noise, and quarrel disappeared together.

We talk of the prospect for a port, and wonder if we are steering for Rio, Pernambuco, Cape Town, or, as some suggest, for "Destruction." Nobody knows, but unless we get a supply of water, the latter seems the most probable.

We have now only a quart for the day, each of us, which is served out at breakfast.

Like quantities of wine, a dollar in money, and various other offers are made for a quart of the precious fluid. It is said the captain sold to a passenger, who represented himself as suffering, a quart of wine for one dollar and a half. The ship's company are unanimous in condemning such petty, unfeeling greediness.

"First mess," again sounds through the ship, signifying the arrival of the dinner hour, and the rush consequent upon this announcement. With dishes in hand, we, perhaps, secure a combination of beans, potatoes, rice, soup, or duff,— a terrific caricature of flour pudding,— in exchange for, or in addition to, our usual beef and bread. These delicacies, on account of narrow cooking accommodations, are furnished only to one mess at once; and those who dislike their meal are thus able to effect a barter with some one in another mess.

Maginnis, the fellow whom we believe a graduate of the Sing-Sing institution, was, somehow, chosen carver of the second-steerage mess, and is guilty of inexcusable partiality;

selecting the best and largest cuts of meat, coupled with slices of duff of equal thickness from the large end of the pudding, which is boiled in a huge bag, of sugar-loaf form, for his particular friends.

This, of course, is the origin of a quarrel, characterized by striking, swearing, and tumbling about the deck. They are separated at last, with bruised and bloody faces, take a saltwater wash, and return to their dishes, only to meet the triumphant shout of the idle gazers, as they find them empty; some sly fellow having stolen their allowance, while they were too busy fighting to care for them.

"Good enough for them," resounds from all sides of the ship, as the poor fellows make their exit with empty plates.

The hours of the afternoon are spent in a manner similar to those of earlier day, with the exception of more sleep. We have work, study, conversation, quarrel, and fighting. Supper is served at sunset, after which comes the best part of the day, made lively by concerts of vocal and instrumental music, public recitations and speeches, entertainments of jokes, narratives, strange delineations of strange events, and sometimes a hornpipe.

As it grows dark, one and another select a "soft place" on the deck, spars, or roof, and prepare to sleep. The song and laugh gradually die away, and by eleven o'clock the ship is still, and nearly all her motley company asleep. A few sit watching the ocean and the sky all the long hours of the night, meditating upon the land and the fortunes they have left behind, or anticipating those in the future.

Payson, the chief mate, has been involved in some disturbance. He is a man of smooth demeanor and plausible speech, but, I verily believe, a thorough and merciless scoundrel. He is a very good friend of mine, however, notwithstanding this indulgence of expression. Being one of those who never go to sea without experiencing seasickness, I was able to administer materially to his comfort during our first rough days out, and he seems, at least, to have the merit of being grateful for favors received.

Signs of rain are manifest. All hands busy in preparing to catch every drop; hoping

SUPPLY OF WATER.

against hope, lest the refreshing draught be denied.

10th.—At two o'clock this morning a heavy squall struck us, and the deck was instantly crowded with people, half dressed, eager to catch the refreshing beverage in every thing that would receive it. In an hour or two we were the happy possessors of two hundred gallons of water—a week's short allowance.

During the day spoke a Spanish brig, bound for Brazil. Only eight casks of water on board, and, of course, none to spare. Crossed the line in the night. Prince Paul seems very ill; is not expected to live.

CHAPTER IV.

PERSONIFICATION OF NEPTUNE. — EFFORTS TO OBTAIN WATER. — JOY ON SEEING LAND. — APPEARANCE OF THE NATIVES. — CATAMARANS, ETC.

11th.— Calm and hot. Towards evening old Neptune came on board, over the bows, after the coarse old fashion, having pretended to hail the ship from afar. This was done by English Charley, one of the crew, personifying his majesty, by fantastically disguising himself with oakum, and various singular devices. This done, he and his train of sea gods forthwith proceeded to administer to the passengers the appropriate rites of naturalization as new subjects of his watery realm.

I was sitting on the quarter deck, talking with the ladies, when these divinities made their appearance. It was the mate's watch, and a good opportunity, as they thought, to carry out their amusement.

The captain, or, indeed, any decent officer,

would have put an end to it at once; for it is, in fact, but an obsolete relic of nautical rudeness, never practiced except on whaling vessels, those disorderly houses of the ocean, or on ships as lawless and ungoverned as our own. Payson, from his station on the quarter deck, kept close watch, permitting them to seize only those who were specially obnoxious, or those to whom he was personally unfriendly or indifferent.

That none might escape, however, they sprinkled a plentiful shower of salt water over every body on deck, and between decks. The unhappy victims of the special operation were subject to a more fearful ordeal, being placed over a tub of water, held firmly down, while a barber-ous operator rubbed tar on their cheeks with a stick, and scraped them with another.

This tonsure accomplished, the ceremony was concluded by upsetting a bucket of sea water on their heads, and setting them at liberty. Some obstinate recusants saved themselves by drawing knives or pistols.

One somewhat contumacious fellow was shaved three times over; at the last escaping to flee toward the cabin, crying "murder," at the top of his voice. As he was descending the stairs, a bucket of salt water was thrown upon his head, mostly received, however, into the face of the captain, who happened to open the door of his room at that moment, for the purpose of ascertaining the cause of the tumult. Of course his anger was aroused, and returning for his pistols, he threatened to fire into the crowd, but finally contented himself with ordering off old Neptune, who immediately obeyed, and thus ended the affair.

The business of practical joking is quite briskly followed up in this ship. One which we infer to be a favorite, from its frequency, is to tie a stout ropeyarn to the feet of some poor fellow asleep on deck, while the other end is carried into the rigging above, continually elevating, slowly and cautiously, till the shoulders only touch the deck. Sleep being impossible in such a situation, and the circumstances tending to kindle the fires of passion, there are usually various contortions, and a burst of profanity at once terrible and amusing. Some lithe, active ones contrive to free themselves;

but almost all have to strive in utter helplessness until they are exhausted, and some tardy but professedly indignant and sympathizing friend comes to the rescue.

Another delicate operation is to tickle the faces of sleepers with a feather suspended from a string, while the unconscious object furnishes the amusement, by his unsuccessful attempts to brush away the supposed creeping thing. It speaks but poorly for our company, when delight in the misery of others is so manifest.

A more amusing spectacle, I venture to say, was never looked upon than we presented a short time since. A barrel of apples were shipped at New York, but were left in the damp air of the hold, where they had been constantly decaying, till the whole was resolved into jelly, as it were, with only here and there a fragment remaining sound. This barrel was brought on deck, and its contents poured into a heap, for the benefit of all whom it might concern. Some twenty men, famishing for any thing of a kindred nature to fruit, instantly threw themselves headlong upon the prize, seeking, with astonishing eagerness, their portion of the inviting pile. I must confess myself as frantic as any body, but instead of trying to dive down through the living mass, I thrust myself under their legs, feeling my way along, and disregarding all manner of knocks and blows.

By this cunning operation in the substratum I quietly selected one apple, and then another, thrusting each within my shirt bosom, until I had gathered more than a dozen, and was obliged, from sheer exhaustion, to make my way out, perfectly covered from forehead to chin, and from chin to lowest extremities, with rotten apple, yet more than repaid, as I thought, for all the trouble and filth, were they ten times as much.

The apples, half crushed and decayed as they were, were as welcome "as apples of gold in pictures of silver;" and strange as it may seem, were unspeakably delicious to the taste.

13th. — Yesterday, the Sabbath, was commenced by the mate prostrating one of the sailors, and leaving him bleeding and senseless upon the deck. How far such a spirit from the design of the seventh day! — a day richer in sacred association than any other that ever dawned upon the human race.

In the morning, with a perfect calm, a party of eight, consisting of passengers and sailors, started in the small boat for a ship four miles distant, with the hope of obtaining some water.

They returned with the report that three hundred gallons might be had, also some wine, at very low rates, but insisted upon stipulating that they alone should return for it, thus indicating some speculative scheme in our necessities.

Upon this, M. Saintpris, one of the French passengers, offered to purchase two or three casks upon his own responsibility, and distribute it among those on board at cost. Speedy assent being given to this, he joined the boat's crew in their return.

Marked indications of a storm appearing late in the afternoon, and the boat not having returned, fears began to be entertained for their safety, which caused the chief mate to man the other boat, and go to their assistance.

Little benefit, however, as it proved. It was

long before either boat returned, and then, amid great darkness, with the wind blowing fearfully, and the crew in both boats stupefied with strong drink. Two whole casks of wine were lost, and only through much difficulty and exertion the third was saved, and the men rescued from their perilous situation. The wine was sold to-day by Saintpris, according to his promise, at one dollar a gallon, being the original cost to him.

The passengers are threatening to make trouble for the captain whenever we get into port, in revenge for his misdemeanors. Prince Paul, however, who has recovered from his sickness, and engaged in his wonted manner, has influenced the leaders to desist in such a movement, by promising a cask of wine — a powerful inducement to them.

We have had another most welcome shower of rain — a matter of great rejoicing, as one would conclude, to see the women and children with cups, teapots, pans, pails, tubs, and indeed every imaginable receptacle, eager to catch the descending drops. A quart of water is a small allowance, in this latitude, for one day, and our supply at this rate is fearfully short.

16th. — We have made another acquisition, acting under the second article of our unwritten code, viz., a case of codfish and a ham. We unobtrusively drew them from the lower hold, which is opened twice a week for the purpose of getting stores, and placed them in a dark corner of our sanctum, whither none are permitted to enter, save our own favored group. Here we have enjoyed many a delicate morsel of codfish and ham, both of which we have eaten raw.

Have spoken ship Duncan Hoyle, from Greenock to Australia. How welcome the sound of these human voices on this wide waste of waters! So much jarring and wrangling, however, within our own limits, an inability to articulate sounds would sometimes seem almost a mercy.

The captain has threatened to kill any one who shall intimate an intention of taking proceedings against him in port for his ill doing.

It is a matter worthy of record, we have had

no fight during the day,—nothing but a *scolding match* between Prince Paul and Terence McManus, an impetuous young Celt, who manifests a purely Irish spirit of independence, advocating strongly every thing opposed to aristocracy, or kindred to it.

He is in almost daily dispute with the Englishmen. The summit of his aspirations seems to be to marshal a company against the captain or some of his officers; but his noisy restlessness and inconsistent conduct, while they furnish considerable amusement, and no little annoyance, are yet the source of very little alarm. The following poetical description is suggested as an epitome of his character:—

> "Each hour a different face he wears;
> Now in fury, now in tears,
> Now laughing, anon in sorrow;
> A while commanding, then obeying;
> Crying for liberty to-day,
> Calling for power to-morrow."

But, evidently, he has a mission, and we have all agreed he was made expressly for the leader of an Irish rebellion; and consequently we have elaborate schemes in contemplation for sending him thither as a pioneer hero in the cause.

17th. — Ill humor sometimes seems a certain result of atmospheric conditions. A peculiarly oppressive and gloomy atmosphere through the day has soured every temper on board; captain, officers, seamen, passengers, and all appeared to be in perfect sympathy with the misanthropic bard, whose productions were of no great weight, but perhaps all we might expect from one so much out of humor with himself and all mankind.

> "*Fret* away, *scold* away;
> Time is going fast;
> Every day is one the less,
> *Scold* on till the last."

Nothing suited any body, unless, indeed, Mrs. Egan was satisfied, as in truth she seemed to be, by wreaking her vengeance upon poor John Newman, the little boasting Englishman.

He had accused her of stealing water from him — no light charge when we are actually suffering from the want of it. This afternoon, as a knot of us were near the hatchway, Newman, all unconscious of his fate, came deliberately up the small ladder. As he stepped on deck, Mrs. E., a stout Irishwoman, with strong right arm, and fearless, violent temper, pounced angrily upon him, jerked him a step forward by the collar, planted him in the midst of the astounded spectators, forthwith instituting the reproachful inquiry, "Stole *wather* from ye, ye miserable *cratur*, hey?" — at the same time giving him two sharp blows with her hand, on either side the head. She gave him no time to recover, but immediately administered, as one of our clerks said, "Ditto, ditto, a size larger," until the poor fellow had endured hard treatment sufficient to shatter his small brains into still more hopelessly small particles.

For a time he seemed inclined to return the blows; but a spectator, scarcely able to speak for his risible emotion, called out, "Strike a woman, will you, you scoundrel!"

This deterred him from the attempt, and led him to seek his escape from the infuriated dame; but her wrath not being fully spent, she refused to let him go. When he was permitted to retire at last, three hearty cheers testified the public appreciation of the effort to maintain the inviolability of female reputation, and also the first article of our admirable code.

The skies and tempers cleared up together towards evening, and after supper we had a pleasant concert, chiefly of instrumental music.

Madam Saintpris, the wife of the French lawyer, who so generously procured us wine, is an accomplished singer, having even appeared with credit at the opera. Several times before she has favored us with solos, which certainly seemed very brilliant to us, and undoubtedly were so.

It is with some measure of appreciation we regard the saying of him who avowed that "music hath charms to rend a rock." What shall we say then of some of our crew, whose hearts seem utterly impervious to these influences?

20th. — We are really in actual suffering. We must inevitably have sickness on board unless we speedily communicate with some friendly vessel or with the shore. Claret has been distributed among us by the supercargo, two quarts of which we may have at one dollar a bottle.

The passengers have been expressing their opinion of the captain's conduct quite freely to-day, even on that ship-master's sanctum, the quarter deck. Becoming somewhat acquainted with the nature of the remarks, he ordered them from the deck; but all in vain he will try to silence these abused and starving men. He may be thankful we do not rise and take the vessel into our own hands. We can count enough sufficiently skilled in navigation to take charge of things, even if every one of the present crew were removed.

Cheese and crackers, and one quart of water a day, is poor cheer after the payments we have made, and the promises we have received; but what is worse, we are told that a pint only will soon be our portion. What we do have is bad, thick, and slimy; but poor as it is, we shall be glad to get such soon.

23d. — Fair breeze, carrying us rapidly to-

PURIFYING THE WATER. 79

wards the coast of Brazil. "Sail ho!" electrified us all, and we anticipated a most seasonable relief. The ship passed quite near us, but our diabolical captain remained obstinately in his cabin, until she was passed, chuckling to himself, probably, at our disappointment, unless he was *spirit*-ually unconscious.

I have conceived some trifling methods to alleviate a little of the discomfort around me, aside from general helpfulness and hopefulness. Having trained myself to drink but little, — no very difficult matter, — I am able to lay by a great part of my allowance. This I place in bottles, which are resting quietly under my mattress. Into each, as I fill it, I drop two or three nails, or a bit of iron, which seems to prove a wholesome correction to the turbid mass. From this store I can dispense, quite frequently, a welcome draught, and have thereby become no small favorite, especially with our fat friend, Mrs. Egan, who is enormously and incessantly thirsty.

In default of a better antisc●●●, I have likewise contrived, by bottling up coffee grounds and boiled tea leaves, to produce a remarkably clear and sharp vinegar, which is keenly relished as a condiment.

25th. — No land yet. All are anxiously watching for it, as our condition is worse daily. Cooked food is but an occasional rarity, and the water is poor enough. Some of us have prepared dried apples, and water caught on deck, producing a miserable, slimy composition, forbidding to both sight and taste under ordinary circumstances, but received with great avidity by many now.

Our comfortless and dangerous situation has not destroyed all our jocularity yet. My roguish companion, Harry Yates, persuaded old man Perrin, as we call him, an honest, simple-hearted countryman, that dried apples, cooked in salt water, were exceedingly promotive of health, especially at sea.

He then charitably volunteered to prepare it for him, and soon had in readiness a nauseous dose, which he administered to his unsuspecting victim, who swallowed no small quantities before he was undeceived, while we were base enough to consider it a funny operation.

27th. — Forty-eight days out. At two this morning, a German boy, who happened to be alone on the bow, saw a low white streak at no very great distance before him. A second look sufficed to confirm his suspicions, and the shout of "Land ho!" resounded through the vessel. Instantaneously the deck was alive with eager gazers at the coast, which, it afterwards appeared, was between Pernambuco and Bahia.

It was scarcely a mile from us, and the vessel was proceeding rapidly in the same direction.

At this moment the captain appeared, and gave orders that the course of the ship be turned as quickly as possible. This quieted the consternation of some of the passengers who were sure of a shipwreck, but scarcely served to cool in any degree the ardor of that tumultuous delight which the welcome sight of land produced in many a heart.

Soon we were sailing through water of a yellowish color, which proved to be the mouth of the River San Francisco. We filled our casks, and felt an unspeakable relief in having something to quench our burning thirst. We keep near as possible to the coast, and our vision, wearied with the monotonous ocean view, finds a pleasing change in the blue mountain ranges in the distance, and the rich green banks that skirt the shore.

Poets may sit down in their quiet homes, and write at their ease of the sublimity and grandeur of " Old Ocean," and that it does present these aspects I do not deny; but let them float upon its wide waste a few months, and that in a miserable bark like ours, and I venture to say their romance would give way before the superior charms of a " cottage in a shady grove," where life and nature are quiet and peaceful, unmingled with the terrors of the briny element.

Soon after we came within sight of land, we discovered something floating in the distance, but were unable to make out what they were.

On approaching nearer, however, we found them to be the " catamarans " of the coast natives, consisting of two logs of fifteen or twenty feet in length, and perhaps two in breadth, lashed together with hide or bark, and crossed in the middle by bars of wood sustaining a basket, in which is kept fishing tackle, bait, and probably the family estate, if they have any. On each of these boats were two natives at least, and sometimes whole families, including men, women, and children. With these rude constructions they often go considerable distances to sea, especially during the pleasant months, floating out with the tide, and paddling about to meet ships, apparently from mere curiosity, having nothing to sell.

Some of our company amused themselves by throwing various things overboard, for the purpose of seeing the Indians dive for them. They had very little clothing, none of them, probably, ever wearing more than the " girdle about the loins."

They live at their ease, find superabundant fruits on shore, catch fish when they desire, and with this simple and plenteous bill of fare, and none for clothing, lodging, or other extras, they live a life free from anxiety and care.

This evening some alarm was again excited by the captain saying that the ship was going ashore in spite of all he could do to the contrary. The chief mate, in a rage, stepped in front of his commander, telling him, if it was his intention to run them ashore, to "say so," and he would prepare for it. No notice was taken of this gross act of insubordination, and the ship was soon righted. Many of us cannot avoid the suspicion that the captain has more than once deliberately attempted to wreck the ship.

CHAPTER V.

LANDING AT BAHIA. — VISIT OF THE CUSTOM-HOUSE OFFICER. — DESCRIPTION OF THE CITY. — VISIT INTO THE COUNTRY. — ENGLISH CHAPEL. — MARKET-PLACES.

31st. — At noon to-day, we came in sight of the lighthouse at the entrance of the Bay of All Saints. Nothing could exceed the joy of the passengers upon finding themselves so near a port. The whole vessel was in commotion, hearty cheers ascending from different companies, and every one almost wild with pleasurable excitement. The scenery on the coast seemed rather rugged at first, but as we came nearer, it grew picturesque and romantic in the extreme. Hills and valleys, shaded with tropical foliage, and feathered with cocoa-nut and palm, refreshed our sight, while here and there we could discover a cottage embowered in trees, whose quiet inmates we imagined a happy people while dwelling securely under their own vines and fig trees.

At 3, P. M., we doubled the cape, and glided into full view of the old Brazilian city of San Salvador, now called Bahia, which lay before us, a "thing of beauty," to our longing eyes. It is built on rising ground, commencing with the business streets near the shore, and extending in rows of dwellings, gardens, groves, and shrubbery, to the bold brows of the bluffs above, upon whose summits we could see convents and cathedrals, hotels and large mansions of more modern style.

We dropped anchor at 4 o'clock, at a point in front of the city, commanding a full view of it, also of the bay, but were not permitted to land, by the custom-house officer who came on board, until morning.

As the shades of evening drew about us, and the solemn music of the convent bells floated out to us over the water, we settled into a calm and quiet mood, feeling more at peace with the world, and with each other, than for a long time before.

We have now accomplished one third of our

long voyage, having reached Bahia, counted from fifteen to twenty-five days' sail from New York, in little less than the sixty days in which it was pretended the whole would be completed. We have, however, endured so much wretchedness, that without adverting to this delay, we find abundant cause for gratitude and delight that we are in port at all.

It is only through divine interposition that we have been repeatedly saved from death by shipwreck and thirst. Our provisions, too, have been fast wasting, and our goods buried in the deep long ago; lightening the ill-stowed and poorly-ballasted ship, so much and so unevenly that we have come into port at Bahia down by the stern, in such a manner that we can dip our handkerchiefs into the water from over the larboard rail.

For a week or two it has been impossible to walk about the deck when wet at all, such was its angle of inclination; thus making our situation one of extreme danger, had we been caught in a heavy blow. Columbus and his crew scarcely felt more joy at the sight of land, than we, poor fellows, at beholding these cliffs before us.

Friday, April 1st.—The captain found himself in trouble at once, at the custom house, for having too many passengers on his list, and only escaped penalty by the help of Consul Gilman. Some one must have informed this officer of the suspicions and charges preferred against the chief mate, for this morning he gave him liberty to leave the vessel, but none to come back.

About nine, the announcement was made by the consul that we might go on shore, and accordingly preparations were made to that effect.

Upon landing we found a few white men; some English and French, who solicited the honor of our patronage for different hotels; but so great was our delight at treading a portion of this mundane earth, that the blue sky above, and the green carpet underneath, seemed well nigh sufficient for man's wants.

Almost all in the streets, however, were negroes; many of them laden with flowers and fruits of the choicest varieties, indescribably tempting to us, after our long confinement to salt and miserable food.

We spent the morning in rambling about the city, with no special object but to see whatever was to be seen. Very little breakfast was eaten on board ship, the proximity of the shore destroying what little appetite remained for wormy bread and mahogany beef. The wants of the "inner man" began to be somewhat clamorous, as my comrade and myself neared a respectable-looking, neatly-arranged French restaurant. "Come, Harry," said I, "we'll have one good dinner if it takes all we've got." We entered, and, for the first time after leaving New York, enjoyed a well-cooked and savory meal.

The table was well set and the bill of fare excellent,—including soup, beef, poultry, sweet potatoes, yams, onions, okra, very good French rolls, claret, and a very fair native wine.

There was also a great variety of fruit for dessert, among which was the blood-red, seedless orange, which I tasted for the first time, and compared with which the best oranges in our northern cities are mere cider apples.

The conclusion of the matter was a bill of three milreas, or nearly two dollars for both, which we paid without grumbling, and resumed our stroll.

The Bay of All Saints is one of the noblest harbors in the world; a magnificent sheet of water of an irregular circle, forty miles in length, and nearly the same in width, affording sheltered anchorage sufficient, it would almost seem, for all the ships in the world. It communicates with the sea by a narrow passage, two miles in length, scarcely one in width, through which we passed.

Bahia is a name given to a maritime province of Brazil, on the eastern coast, extending from about 9° to 15° 45′ south latitude. The estimate of its area varies with different individuals, some placing it at fifty-four thousand square miles, and others at ninety-seven thousand; the latter, however, mostly credited.

Statements with regard to population also differ; probably amounts to about seven hundred thousand. Bays and inlets abound along the coast, among the most celebrated of which is All-Saints Bay. Numerous rivers traverse the province; the Rio San Francisco, the largest, or one of the largest, of the Brazilian rivers, flowing along its north-west frontier.

The cultivation of tobacco is peculiar to the province, and its produce much sought after, not only for the market of Portugal, but also for Spain and the whole of Barbary.

The soil is also admirably adapted to the cultivation of the sugar cane; and the sugar of this province is considered of superior quality — a circumstance finding sufficient proof in the fact that Bahia alone exports more of this article than all the rest of Brazil.

An annual increase of the cotton growth shows Bahia to be fast becoming a formidable rival to Pernambuco. Rice of a fine quality is among her productions, and coffee, much excelled, however, by that of Rio de Janeiro.

This province was one of the first peopled by Europeans, and it is also one of those, it is said, from which they have most effectually removed all traces of the original inhabitants.

Bahia, or San Salvador, where we now are, is the capital of the above province, situated immediately within Cape St. Antonio, which forms the right or east side of this noble Bay of All Saints.

It was founded about 1549 by Thomas de Souza, first captain-general of Brazil, and was until 1763 the capital of the colony. Since that period Rio has been acknowledged as the capital.

It is one of the largest and most important cities of South America, though inferior to its rival in population and commercial importance.

Its population is estimated from 120,000 to 160,000, of which a third are supposed to be whites, the same number mulattoes, and the remainder blacks.

It is built partly along the ridge, and partly on the declivity of a very high and steep hill, fronting the entrance of the bay; and in the number and beauty of its public buildings, ranks among the first cities of Brazil.

Among the most noticeable is the cathedral, once the church of the Jesuits, dedicated to San Salvador, and considered the handsomest ecclesiastical building in the country. It is built of European marble; its interior richly decorated, containing two portraits — one of

Ignatius Loyola and San François Xavier—which are regarded as rare specimens of art.

The theater is built upon a rock, more than a thousand feet above the level of the sea; but as the slope northward, toward the suburbs, is quite gradual, and a greater part of those who patronize the theater come from thence, the inconvenience is not great. Indeed, most of the largest and finest buildings are upon high points quite difficult of access.

In the lower part of the town is the Exchange, a massive building of modern date, built in a peculiar style, an attempted imitation of the Grecian. The houses are mostly built of stone, and contrary to the usual practice in South America, many consist of three, four, and even five stories. The principal street is the Praya, in which is situated the Church of the Conception, remarkable on account of the stones which compose its structure having been prepared and numbered in Europe, and brought in two frigates; so that upon their arrival they had merely to be arranged in the order previously allotted to them.

A public library is shown of some sixty thousand or seventy thousand volumes, among which are a few ancient Portuguese works, and some manuscripts; but the greater portion are in French.

As a city, however, it can boast of very few institutions devoted to intellectual culture, and these are under the control of bigoted ecclesiastics, who care little, and do less, for the advancement of educational systems.

Bahia is a place long celebrated for its ship building. As late as 1824, some of the finest ships that graced the seas were built at this port.

The modes of traveling strike one as novel and peculiar, the vehicle, being a sort of palanquin, supported by negroes, who make a practice of clustering about the corners of the streets, with the hope of having their services called in requisition in that direction. In carrying people from one part of the city to another, the "silla" is in general use; which is nothing more than a stout wooden chair, strapped to the shoulders of a man, in which one seats himself, and is transported whithersoever he will, provided suitable inducements are offered.

Weary of wandering when night began to think of unfolding her mantle, and feeling some solicitude as to a resting place for the hours of darkness, I turned boldly to the best hotel in the city, where I found several of the ship's company, and among them Mr. Payson. While lounging about in a hesitating manner, he asked what lodgings I had secured, and upon my replying, "none," he invited me to remain, and he would be responsible for my bills. I was truly grateful, and thanked him most sincerely, thinking it a rich reward for small acts of kindness done to a sick ship's officer.

Verily,—
"A little word mildly spoken,
A little deed kindly done,"

insures its own rich fund of blessing.

April 7th.— Some of our company engaged a boarding place in the country for the time of our stay in port, necessarily having an eye to economy, and also for the purpose of avoiding the unhealthy exposures of the city.

Comfortably settled in their new abode, our little company were invited to visit them. Mules are often used in traveling, especially by the wealthier classes, who have heavy carriages drawn by six or eight of these animals; but preferring a cheaper and less showy equipage, we availed ourselves of our own powers of locomotion by starting on foot.

We left the city by the western road, and followed the shores of the bay for a mile, enjoying the surf, and the vast cabinet of shells, arranged after Nature's own model. We passed the residences of many of the wealthy people of the city, who seemed to be living in luxurious splendor in their fashionable retirement.

Many of the finest were in process of renovation, their mosaic walks of shell work being laid in cement; and marble vases, variegated stone flower pots, statuary, &c., being refitted or replaced by new; which, with corresponding interior decorations, would make palaces worthy of kings."

We journeyed at leisure over gently undulating hills, past fields of sugar cane, and shady

BRAZILIAN COUNTRY SEAT

- 4 -

groves of plantain and cocoa nut; fairly reveling in the heavy perfume from fruit and flowers, wafted to us on the morning breeze from over the bay.

Suddenly emerging from a thicket, we came in full view of a ridge, upon whose summit stood a long row of one-story, white buildings, the country seat of our fellow-voyagers. Their special home was a neat, airy cottage, snugly planted in a grove of orange and lemon trees.

The scene was one of great magnificence. The front view afforded a near glance of the city; of rich and smiling valleys; while in the further distance was the vast expanse of the beautiful bay.

The slope in the rear was laid out in fine gardens, stretching down to the valley, intersected by winding paths, ornamented with shells and stones of various colors, inlaid with innumerable devices, and these still farther embellished with statuary, urns, and flower vases. Farther down were the little hamlets of the natives; and here and there a fruit orchard, cocoa grove, or vegetable garden.

The little fleet of ships in port were motionless, with furled sails, with the exception of one or two gliding on their course before a light breeze.

Still discernible in the distance was the small steamer, that had left Bahia for the purpose of conveying to their chosen location a company of Massachusetts farmers, who have been induced to come to this country with their wives, children, flocks, herds, and implements, with the professed object of introducing agricultural improvements.

The Brazilian government, it seems, not only gives land, but money, to those who will enlist in this enterprise of native cultivation.

This party, we are told, receive quite a handsome salary, both men and women, the latter being requested to establish a dairy, if possible.

Perhaps it was the knowledge of this delegation that suggested the idea to some of our number of abandoning the voyage to Australia, and seeking employment in the diamond mines of Brazil.

The insane project, however, proved a failure, fortunately for them; for, even supposing government would have permitted them to enter those remote and guarded realms, and they had not perished in the vast wilderness on the way, there would only have remained the splendid contingency of freedom, a cheap suit of clothes, and a few dollars, if they should be successful in finding a stone of so many carats.

But to return from this digression to the description of our visit; we sat a long time in front, lost in the beauty of the glorious landscape, before we were aroused by summons to partake of refreshments on the other side of the house.

Repairing to the spot, we found a table spread in the shade, decorated with flowers, and filled with oranges, cocoa nuts, guavas, dates, figs, bananas, mangoes, bread, water, wine, dried fruits, coffee, and cigars.

Completely embowered in roses, oleanders, and geraniums; shaded by the rich foliage of the tropical trees; waited on by a bevy of neatly-dressed brown girls, we sat long at the feast, as at one seldom to be enjoyed. After a short *siesta* of two hours, we awoke to take a stroll through the grounds. Our agreeable host, it appeared, had arranged a dance and picnic under the trees by moonlight. Guests from neighboring plantations began to arrive at nine, and at ten the musicians struck up a lively air, that set the pretty *senoritas* to dancing in earnest. The guitar seems to be their favorite instrument, and its low, sweet tones were particularly pleasing at this time.

The faint light of morning was visible when the company dispersed; and thus ended a day and night which many hardships and present pleasures conspired to render so full of pleasure, that then and now it were more like an enchanted dream than a thing of reality.

11th. — Yesterday, some of us attended divine service for the first time since leaving New York. Wishing to make a respectable appearance, and having no other decent garments, we arrayed ourselves in the heavy woolen suits in which we started from home in the middle of winter, but found our coats quite too cumbersome before we had proceeded far.

Our way led us by the Park, situated on the

bluff, commanding a beautiful prospect of the bay and the business streets of the city. As we looked in, and saw the ground strewed with ripe oranges, seats arranged most invitingly under the trees, we felt inclined to take advantage of our early start, in the quiet enjoyment of the scene.

The day was oppressively hot, even for Bahia. We seated ourselves in as comfortable a posture as possible, divesting ourselves of hats, shoes, &c.; but scarcely had we finished our arrangements, ere one of the numerous half soldier, half policemen,—who swarm about the city with hot-looking uniforms of black, red, and green, bearing sword and musket,— presented himself, discharging a lot of Brazilian Portuguese, among which was distinguishable, "*Baya! baya! Vamos! vamos! Malo! malo!*" signifying, in general, that we were violating their laws, and must depart.

Some were ready to go, and others, unwilling, pretended not to understand.

"*Baya! baya! Vamos!*" repeated the officer, pointing to the gate. Finding them still incorrigible, he hailed a brother official, who came up in an ireful, threatening manner, inspiring the feeling that it were better to leave, since we could not afford to offer bribes, and the stern virtue of the policemen is blind and deaf to every thing else.

From the Park, a handsome, straight street leads more than a mile back to Victoria Square. Both the street and the square are lined with fine houses, to which are attached large and magnificent gardens, belonging to English and foreign residents, of whom there are two hundred and more, mostly engaged in commercial houses and the shipping business.

The English Chapel, newly erected by the British government, is a small, modest building, in the square, almost lost sight of in the dense foliage of the trees which surround it. We entered its courts gladly, and joined in the responses of the service with great satisfaction. Long deprivation prepared us to appreciate the sensible discourse of the clergyman — a man of middle size, with kindly expression, pleasing manners, who preached from the text, "And he did it not from the fear of God."

K., a smart young fellow, whom we call

the "ship's lawyer," complained of his head on his way to the chapel. He continued to grow worse, and on our return to the hotel wished me to call a physician immediately, as he was quite confident he had the yellow fever, and should survive but a short time. Reason evidently was tottering, and I sought medical advice, but received only the information that it was a sunstroke, and by gratifying his whims he might soon be better. This made no difference with K., who surely thought it his last sickness. He gave me his watch, with the request that I should give it to his father whenever I should reach the United States, made disposition of his remaining effects, and with a serious and resigned countenance, said, "Now I am ready; the fever will take me away soon." He retained his delusion for some time, constantly imploring to be carried to the hospital, that he might die.

Such was his earnestness, we went through the usual forms of application, taking care, however, that the actual result should not be secured. This has proved a sad disappointment to the sufferer, but we have thought it best, and shall do all we can for his comfort ourselves. No improvement manifest to-day.

14th. — We spend our days at Bahia, in rambling about; sometimes along the bay to the westward; sometimes over the north point of the harbor and up the sea coast, and again through the churches and public buildings of the city.

In case we should feel disinclined to return at evening, we provide ourselves with lunch, expecting to find a luxurious dessert in the tropical fruits which we take from the ground as abundantly and innocently as we should walnuts and chestnuts in West Hartford woods; while for lodging we seek entrance into some Indian hut. Usually, however, the hotel is the place of rendezvous for the night, where I sleep soundly on the floor, with two newspapers for my mattress, and lizards for my attendants.

One who does not see' the market place does not see the half of Bahia. A new and spacious edifice of stone is being erected for the accommodation of this portion of the public,

GREEN LIZARD

but it is little advanced; and in the mean while the area of the square is thickly covered with wooden sheds, irregularly set, in which the venders appear — a numerous and motley company of negro slaves, free blacks, and native Brazilians, of every shade of black and brown, offering every conceivable thing; not only meats, but every variety of flowers, fruit, and vegetables; dry goods, groceries, hardware; in short, every sort of commodity procurable in the city, except, perhaps, some fine cloths. We find inexhaustible amusement in examining the varieties of country produce; watching the strings of mules and donkeys that bring it in; having thus a fine opportunity to study the manners and national peculiarities of the people.

Most of us young fellows have struck up a sort of trade acquaintance with one and another of the more comely brown girls at the fruit stands. They have acquired from customers a few English words, which they use promiscuously, spicing freely with a jovial *ki-hi* style of African laughter. As they perceive us coming, each jumps at her special customer, seizes him unceremoniously by the arm, jokes away her competitors; never releasing her hold until all her English and his Portuguese are exhausted, and a dump or two is invested in her special commodities.

By far the most striking of the market women are the pure negroes, some of whom are native Africans, still bearing the characteristics of their tribe.

The Brazilian negroes almost seem like caricatures of their brethren in the United States, so much more exuberant are they in spirits, and in extravagant and fantastic costumes.

For dress patterns, the ladies of the market usually select furniture calico, with large red and yellow figures; adorn them with flounces, edgings of coarse lace a foot in width, or some of those styles of heavy ball or tassel fringe which we use for curtains.

The head dress is a gaudy Madras handkerchief, when the hair is not carded out and arranged with flowers.

We have actually seen the last painful operation performed with leather and wooden cards, not unlike those used at home, instead of currycombs, on less sensitive animals.

My own especial favorite and great admiration is a sable Amazon, weighing at least three hundred pounds — a fat and expansive creature, almost as black and shiny as patent leather; with a round face, almost as radiant, in spite of its color, as a full moon; clear, white eyes, with large jetty pupils, that may have broken many an Ethiopian heart; a mouth filled with pearly teeth; and, withal, so invariably and joyously smiling, that she was positively delightful in conversation.

She dresses in the hight of fashion — usually in a dress of white, bordered with a heavy flounce, trimmed with gay flowers and variously-colored ribbons, and an enormous calla and japonica in her hair.

She sits upon her throne, evidently, with as much satisfaction as the proudest empress, in her coronet of jewels; rejoicing in the gorgeous display of flowers and fruit around her; receiving patronage from many merely for the sake of gazing at her gigantic ebony proportions.

The inhabitants, whether Indians, negroes, or Europeans, have invariably treated us with extreme politeness and great hospitality. The policemen often hail us when returning to the city in the evening; but a little explanation in English, ending with *amigo*, always suffices to give us undisturbed passage.

We were soon recognized as law-abiding persons; but it is true, if we did not fear their unscrupulous perquisitions of all sorts of bundles and parcels, we should carry more private stores of fruit with us than we shall now dare to do.

Among the class of boatmen is John, a smart, good-natured negro, whom we have often employed, and whose heart we have occasionally rejoiced by giving him a dime instead of the usual fare — a *dump*, which is a copper coin, about the size of an English penny. His gratitude always finds expression in a form of acknowledgment learned of the English sailors, ignorant of its application, and therefore more sincere than complimentary, we think; viz., "You one fine d—d fool." So much for the tendency of human nature to acquire that which is evil.

CHAPTER VI.

ROMANCE OF A WALK IN THE TROPICAL REGION. — DIFFICULTIES IN LEAVING PORT. — HISTORY OF BRAZIL. — NARROW ESCAPE FROM FIRE.

THE beauty and luxuriance of tropical vegetation can scarcely be conceived by those accustomed to the comparatively sterile regions of the temperate zone. The dense foliage of the trees, the almost impenetrable forests, are rather more agreeable in the prospect, however, than while testing their convenience by actual experiment. In order to give the reader a faint idea of these things, I sketch a description of a walk, before proceeding to the next date on record, which my companion and myself proposed, with the intention of making a circuit through the woods, coming out some distance inland, upon the shore of the bay. After leaving the marble-walled or iron-railed enclosures of the great suburban gardens, the country is, to a good extent, of apparently primeval forest, altogether without fences, yet dotted here and there, at long intervals, with a sugar plantation, or Indian village, with the accompanying orchards and gardens. Mere foot paths are winding about, not so wide or distinct as those which usually intersect the woods of New England, sometimes leading *somewhere*, but oftener *nowhere*. We started long before sunrise, and plunged into the depths of the forest, pursuing our devious and intricate way through such paths as these, worn only by human feet. On and still on we went, looking with wonder at the enormous trees, from which drooped equally large vines, all of which were twined and intertwined with masses of flowers; regaled at the same time with the sweet, melodious notes of innumerable birds, the better to represent which, were I a naturalist, and desirous of celebrity, I should probably define, with a list of certain unpronounceable names, that would look very scientific, to say the least.

These heavy vines seemed to extend miles in succession, actually adorning whole forests with festoons of flowers; realizing the most extravagant pictures of romance, provided we say nothing of the lizards, and chattering monkeys that glided and leaped about us.

The air was thick with the almost suffocating perfumes of flowers, and alive with the hum of numberless insects, so that, in the intoxication of our senses, we lost our way. Hoping to reach the bay at some familiar point, we went forward, pushing our way with difficulty through shrubs, vines, and broad leaves; often obliged to make a road with our pocket knives; our Yankee blood telling handsomely in our favor the while. Finding it an utterly fruitless attempt to beat a path upon the ground, we walked, or rather scrambled, over a sort of "airy" course, formed by stems, vines, and flowers, coming nearer than ever before to the fanciful period of life — "a path with roses strewed." We at last succeeded in forcing our way down a steep hill, over half a mile of swamp, which stretched across the valley, and reached an open space on the opposite side. We regretted our hard-fought passage on one account, as it compelled us to drop many curious flowers, and rare specimens of vegetation, retaining only a few seeds, and some pods of wild cotton, apparently of superior quality.

Feeling now quite at ease by a knowledge of our relation to the points of compass, we made a hearty meal of bread and dried fruit; after which we enjoyed a most refreshing *siesta* under the shadow of the broad plantain.

Awaked from this, we pursued our journey over the hill, coming quickly upon a deserted plantation, whose dilapidated walls spoke convincingly of the withering touch of Father Time. This we imagined to have been the residence of some wealthy family during the palmy days of San Salvador. Such, indeed, were the indications — as ruined statuary, marble fountains, and bathing places: relics of elaborate carving and massive stone-work, were still visible.

A few families of natives were living about, possibly the descendants of the former slaves of the establishment; the proprietor having been compelled by misfortune, or political change, to flee from his charming home.

These poor people, nevertheless, represented well the ancient hospitalities of the domain, treated us with even ceremonious politeness, and when we wished to depart, kindly showed us a path to the city, which we were glad to avail ourselves of, being weary with the day's adventure, though prosecuted in the midst of objects of singular beauty and attractiveness.

We enjoyed keenly this delightful land, with scarcely a thought either for the past or the future, notwithstanding the web of troubles and fatalities woven about our "beautiful clipper" were as tangled as ever, as will be seen by date of twenty-first April, twenty-one days after our arrival at Bahia.

No steps being taken to prepare for the continuation of the voyage, and being generally agreed that it should not be broken up if possible, a meeting of the passengers has been called, at which they considered the matter of using the Peytona as the private property of the passengers until our safe arrival in Australia, and full reimbursement of all expenses incurred on the ship's account. A committee was appointed to represent the state of the ship to the consul, Mr. Gilman, who answered that his strict legal duty was to send the

Peytona back to New York, for the violation of passenger laws, and irregular papers. This, they gave him to understand, was scarcely practicable, as they were fixed in their determination to proceed, though they should work the vessel themselves. Upon this the consul advised the captain to advertise for the requisite means, as this is the plea, which he accordingly did; and some gentlemen were found who were disposed to negotiate in the matter, but found, on inquiry, that no responsible owner appeared, which put an end to the plan at once.

A second effort was made by the captain, in which he proposed to the passengers to raise the sum of fifteen hundred dollars, as the responsibility of getting out from port rested upon them; but they only gave what Rev. Mr. Abbott says must be given to all street beggars — "frowns and flat denials." The money might as well be thrown into the sea.

In this uncertain condition sickness has begun to manifest itself, which has finally assumed the fearful type of yellow fever, aided probably by the free use of tropical fruits, and manner of living.

Park, a stalwart man, forty years of age, has died on board. He lay neglected upon the deck nearly a week previous to his death, and although at the time fifty persons were within twenty yards of him, no one knew when the "King of Terrors" came. Such is the apathy and indifference to each other's welfare into which the passengers have fallen, though, doubtless, fear of infection influenced more or less.

Fowler, the blaspheming Vermonter, who prayed so vehemently in our first gale, was taken the same evening, and died soon after. A Polish count, one of our foreign shipmates, has also fallen a victim.

With such danger in our midst, the ship's debt daily increasing, and the chances of leaving port diminishing in the same ratio, a last and more energetic effort has been made to raise the money; for bills must be paid, as the authorities are strict in preventing the departure of any vessel in debt. A statement of grievances was made, concluding with a request that the ship might be fitted out and sent to sea, and the same put into the hands of the consul. He seemed anxious to aid us, but could do nothing till bills were met. Accordingly, fifteen hundred dollars were obtained in contributions of from five to two hundred dollars, some having sold their watches and other valuables for the purpose of obtaining the desired amount, and the whole appropriated by Mr. Gilman to the cancellation of the ship's demands. This has so incensed the captain that he came on board threatening never to leave port unless three thousand dollars were raised and placed at his own disposal.

No notice was taken of his senseless threats, but of course it causes detention, and many of us are beginning to feel that our present mode of life is not altogether the thing, however pleasant it may be.

29th. — After various hinderances we are once more at sea, having been on board some time, with the daily hope and expectation of leaving port. We weighed anchor in the morning, but the afternoon only afforded us sufficient breeze to make any progress. For a time matters appeared dubious indeed. As a British sloop of war, with her schooner consort, was seeking to intercept our course, for the obvious reason that we had a deserter from each. Upon nearing us they signified their desire to search the ship, and were given full permission by our commander, who gravely asserted no such men were on board, though at the very hour he knew perfectly well the place of their secretion. After some little hesitation they turned their course, leaving us to pursue our quiet way. And now that we are fairly out, and are rid of some of our worst characters, we have hopes of completing our voyage in comparative comfort. Eleven of our original company are left behind, among whom are the chief mate, our thievish steward, Prince Paul, and several others, who await a fairer opportunity of prosecuting their voyage.

Grant is our first mate, and "Big George," our first volunteer, the second.

We have water, and a considerable stock of fresh provisions, which the consul and committee together put on board, and made the captain acknowledge as bought for the vessel, before they were paid for. Many, like myself, have private stores of fruit, and such miscellaneous articles as our means would enable us to procure at Bahia.

30th. — Rough weather. The captain is evidently trying to make himself agreeable; instituting inquiries in different parts of the ship whether all are comfortable; if any thing is wanting, or wrong; but we, who have endured so much in the past, are little inclined to cordiality.

A magazine has been discovered below, well stored with fire-arms and various sorts of ammunition; knowledge of which has called out a vigilance committee, composed of the same men who have hitherto been the most prominent in all organized action, and are supported by the most intelligent and reliable of the passengers. Some one or more of these are on deck, night and day, watching the condition and progress of things in general, and ready to rally assistance at once, in case of an outbreak. In order to prevent theft, it has likewise been enacted that thieves, when detected, shall be posted upon the mizzenmast.

One of our deserters, it appears, is a "sergeant of marines" from the English sloop of war, and the other a sailor from the schooner; both strong, large men, and, withal, smart. The former came on board through the influence of one of our men, whom he met in the city; it being considered a point of honor with a common sailor to help on a deserter. The latter, however, had more to encounter. He quietly let himself down from the schooner, with his clothes attached, in a parcel, with the intention of swimming to the ship, a distance of two miles and a half — a feat he would have performed had he not forgotten the ebb tide in his calculations, which carried him in a different direction from that he desired.

He shouted so loudly, he was heard, taken up, and brought on board the Peytona, at his own request, and is now at work with the men in the forecastle, it being the usual practice to dispose of them thus in such cases. The sergeant is a waiter in the first cabin.

May 1st. — I avail myself of the first opportunity to consider the history of Brazil in general, giving its most important features, as I obtained them from authentic sources. Nothing awakens a deeper interest in a country than having visited it. Accounts of travelers then become invested with special interest, since comparisons are instituted, and the truth tested by actual knowledge. Such is my interest in the Brazilian empire, though personally acquainted with only a portion of it. This vast tract, second only in extent to the great empires of China and Russia, stretches along about two thirds of the east coast of South America, while its superficial area occupies nearly half its whole extent. The country formerly included under the name of Brazil appears to have been much more limited in extent; but the Portuguese, ambitious of new acquisitions, have continually added to their possessions, which have been confirmed to them, from time to time, by treaties with Spain.

About two thirds of the country is high land and mountains; the highest range of which traverses the center, and is of an altitude of six thousand feet.

The coast range, or Serra do Mar, is by far the most picturesque of the Brazilian chains, approaching in some parts within sixteen or eighteen miles of the sea, while in others it sweeps inland to a distance of one hundred and twenty to one hundred and forty miles.

The soil near the coast displays evidences of the richest cultivation, teeming with abundance of the choicest productions. The ancient forests, which have been noticed, whose giant trees, and countless plants and shrubs, so thickly interwoven as almost to defy the attempts of man to force a passage, sufficiently attest the great fertility of the soil on which they grow.

But the soil as well as the climate exhibits different phases in different parts of the country, being modified, in a great measure, by certain natural conditions. The seasons may very properly be styled " the wet and the dry," though some divide them into four; the spring commencing in September, the summer in December, the autumn in March, and the winter in June.

Langsdorff, the former Russian consul at Rio, remarking upon the seasons of Brazil, says, " Winter, in this country, resembles summer in the north of Europe ; summer appears one continuous spring, while spring and autumn are unconsciously lost in winter and summer." It may therefore be said of this country, with more propriety than of any other, that —

> " Stern winter smiles on this auspicious clime ;
> The fields are florid in eternal prime ;
> From the bleak pole no winds inclement blow,
> Mold the round hail, or flake the fleecy snow ;
> But from the breezy deep the groves inhale
> The fragrant murmurs of the eastern gale."

The most celebrated, though not the most important, of the natural productions, are diamonds; the most noted mine being that of Serra do Frio. This district is surrounded by almost inaccessible rocks, and was formerly guarded with so much vigilance that not even the governor of the province had the liberty of entering it without the special permission of the director of the mines.

The mines are usually wrought during the hot season, at a time when the beds of the rivers and torrents are dry, and the diamond sand can be easily extracted. The operation of washing is deferred till the wet season, and is performed in the open air, or frequently under sheds where the action of the sun is least likely to injure the health of those concerned. It is said to be a rare thing that one discovers more than two or three diamonds of seventeen or twenty carats weight in the course of a year, and one may labor twice that period without finding one of thirty carats weight.

Down to the date of 1771 the right of working the mines was farmed out, but since that time the government have taken it into their own hands, and they are all under the superintendence of a board. The crown receive one fifth of the total value.

Gold also exists, though the greater portion of the supposed mines remain untouched. The most celebrated is that of Congo Loco, situated in a beautiful valley, at the distance of some forty leagues from Villarica. Bethencourt, a Portuguese, was the first person who commenced working these mines with his own hands, in 1740, and soon amassed a splendid fortune. His descendants disposed of them, and finally they came into the possession of a company of Englishmen, known as the " Anglo-

Brazilian Mining Company," for ten thousand pounds sterling.

The eagerness of all classes to engage in mining pursuits, proved a great obstacle to the improvement of the country, for a long time. This rage having subsided in a great measure, the energies of the people have been directed to the safer and infinitely more productive occupations of the soil, so that the value of gold and diamonds is quite inconsiderable now, compared with that of various other articles.

Sugar and coffee are the staple products of the country, and the culture of these has increased with wonderful rapidity; and such is the facility for commercial intercourse, that the development of her resources may be constantly and powerfully accelerated. Perhaps no country is more favored by nature, as regards the requisites for carrying on an extensive commerce, than Brazil.

All its principal cities are on the coast: its harbors are among the finest in the world, and are connected with the interior by many large rivers, most of which are navigable for a considerable way inland.

One lamentable feature in the history of the country is a great want of schools, there being no means by which even the children of the middle classes can acquire any thing like a really useful education.

It was not until 1808 that a printing press was introduced, and a newspaper established. Several publications are now issued, but, as may be supposed, literature has few charms, and is likely to find but little improvement among such a people.

The established religion is the Roman Catholic; all other religions, however, being tolerated.

Considering the period during which Brazil has been colonized, its vast extent and fertility, the variety of its productions, and its favorable situation for commerce, its progress in the accumulation of wealth and population has been very slow. Many circumstances combine to bring about such a result; such as, " the principles by which it was governed by the mother country; the oppressive restrictions laid on the trade and industry of the colonists, and, more than all the rest, the ignorance of the Portuguese, and their inferiority, in respect to science and art, to most other nations of Europe.

A brighter day is already dawning, and the future may yet witness more rapid strides in civilization than has yet been seen in the history of any other people.

12th. — A young man, twenty-three years of age, died to-day of *delirium tremens*. He was an active, healthy fellow on leaving New York, but indulged freely in the intoxicating beverage on the way out, and during his stay at Bahia. Soon after we set sail, he was haunted night and day by the fiendish sights and sounds of his disease, and his terrific groans filled the ship. Last evening seemed to bring an abatement of the delirium, and he appeared on deck, very weak, and fully conscious that he was dying — a conviction which brought him under the influence of rational but even more appalling fears. He warned all about him to beware of a similar course, and left this world entreating us, with his last breath, to pray for him. This dreadful death, and the solemnity of our first ocean burial, evidently produces a profound impression; but I fear it will prove transient, and the memory of the dead and his misery be effaced, without any transforming power upon those who so much need to feel it.

June 1st. — Weather warm and calm. The main object of the passengers seems to be to pass away time as comfortably as possible, and for this purpose the most shady places are selected, and retained not only during the day, but till day dawns again. A sudden shower, during the night, occasionally causes great commotion. Most of those on deck follow their first impulse and rush to the companion way to escape a drenching, for a shower in the tropics is a genuine "opening of the floodgates." Some cool and deliberate individuals, however, like my friend Harman, remain unmoved through it all. While trying to persuade him to leave his watery bed for one more desirable in the cabin, he gave a faint groan, and without opening his eyes, replied, "O, don't disturb me, if you please, I'm so comfortable."

Four months ago, nothing but the softest bed would have sufficed for him; now he can take special comfort on a board, in a heavy rain storm. So much for the power of adaptation to circumstances.

There is a wonderful fascination in sailing upon the ocean, before a gentle breeze, by the clear moonlight. But beautiful as are the rays of Luna, it is nevertheless dangerous to gaze upon them unveiled, in the tropics. Some of us paid no attention to the warnings of the old sailors, and slept on deck with face and eyes exposed, but have been visited, in consequence, with swollen faces and sore eyes, accompanied with singular nervous irritation, and involuntary twitching of the muscles — a state of things produced, as our oracles say, by being "frost-bitten by the moon."

So are some of the keenest delights of this sublunary sphere mingled with almost death-fraught evils; reminding us of the folly of placing hopes of happiness on any of the untrue things this side heaven.

2d. — This morning had a long call from a

great right whale, almost as long as the ship. It played about us in the most friendly manner, apparently under the impression that we were another whale, and our acquaintance desirable. Had we been the fortunate owners of a harpoon, we might have unpleasantly undeceived him.

No signs of land yet, although thirty-five days out from Bahia; the average voyage from this latter port to Cape Town being only twenty-eight days. None seem to know where we are.

The captain keeps all in ignorance with respect to longitude. He has been navigating in the most perverse manner, actually having steered days at a time north, south, east, and west, and every possible intermediate course, since leaving Brazil, as if sailing all over the Atlantic to find the cape.

Frivolous reasons are sometimes given for such conduct, and sometimes none at all. Many are confident of an intention to wreck us on the coast of South America, with an eye to securing the insurance of fourteen thousand dollars upon the ship.

The captain has issued repeated threats of late that he will destroy us in some way or other, even intimating an intention to set fire to the magazine. This aggravated outrage is doubtless occasioned by our having forced him, as we did, to leave Bahia.

11th. — This morning, as we were running eastward at the rate of eight miles an hour, in the midst of a dense fog, we were startled by the cry of "Land ho! Directly ahead." As the mist was dissipated before the rising sun, the rocky coast of Africa loomed up a few miles before us. The ship was immediately put about to the south-west, and thus we were again rescued from imminent peril; or, as I believe, from a diabolical scheme against the ship and all within her.

For several hours stumps of trees and green branches floated by us on the water, indicating we were off the mouth of some river, probably the Orange. While indulging in the anticipations of seeing land, a cry of "Fire!—the ship is all on fire in the hold!" resounded through the ship, which was followed by a general rush for the upper deck. In order to preserve room for action, those above had removed the ladder, which increased the fright to a perfect frenzy, inasmuch as a column of flame came leaping up at the instant, filling the whole hatchway. Mysteriously to myself I gained the deck, in season to hear "Big George," our second mate, exclaim, in a commanding voice, "Do as I tell you, and I'll save your lives."

The calm self-possession of the man, in such an emergency, instantly secured him the implicit obedience of all. Busy hands were speedily at work passing water, with all the rapidity that mortal fear could inspire; but nearly an hour elapsed before the flames were sufficiently subdued to think of descending.

At the end of that time the bold mate went down amid the black smoke and charred freight, creeping about in the confined hold among the cinders, suffocating atmosphere, and struggling fire, distributing here and there buckets of water that were passed to him, until every vestige of a spark disappeared.

Anson Carrington, the steward, also merits

particular credit for his intrepidity, in saving us from danger at this fearful crisis. In the midst of the tumult the cry was heard, "The fire will reach the magazine!" While others seemed paralyzed, he darted to the dangerous spot, and in several attempts, succeeded in depositing the ammunition in a place of comparative safety on a distant part of the deck.

It was long before quiet was restored, but with it came many speculations as to the origin of the fire. A searching investigation was held, resulting in the revelation that one of the ship's boys had been in the practice of stealing through the place with a lamp, for the purpose of obtaining some liquor; and being frightened, had dropped it, and thereby occasioned our distress. As a sort of penalty, he has been confined; but the jolly songs that he sings is proof that his imprisonment is any thing but irksome to him. There is indignant talk, but the seamen are under no control, and we dare not meddle with them, neither the captain nor mates; and the only practicable course seems to be, to keep on the right side of them, if possible, and get along as easily as we can. Our escape is even more wonderful than our preservation from shipwreck. Had the liquor casks taken fire, no human power could have saved the ship, and scarcely, by any possibility, the lives; having but two boats, and those in a miserable condition.

The ship, which was headed toward the land at the first alarm, has once more been laid on her course; and the confusion of weeping and congratulation, wonder and inquiry, has succeeded · to the agonizing screams of the two hours passed on the confines of a fearful death.

This is another signal interposition of Providence in our favor, yet no one says any thing of thankfulness for our deliverance. The many vicissitudes we have experienced, the hardships and dangers encountered, so far from inciting us to right action, have, as it were, crusted our minds with a sort of insensibility to all considerations except those of the present moment. Memory, gratitude, and hope have alike grown dim with us all.

CHAPTER VII.

A LUNAR BOW. — TERRIFIC STORM. — LANDING AT CAPE TOWN. — RAMBLES ABOUT THE CITY. — IMPRISONMENT OF THE CAPTAIN. — VISIT TO SEYOLA, THE KAFFIR CHIEF. — A PRAYER MEETING ON SHIPBOARD.

15th. — A calm, clear, and beautiful day. Early this morning R. F., of New York, a young man of twenty-six, came to his death by disease caused by dissipation at Bahia. He was a merry, lively fellow, with a smile and a joke for every one; and his early, unhappy death has thrown a shade of melancholy over every body. After breakfast, all assembled to pay the last tribute of respect to his mortal remains, and witness his burial in the great cemetery of the deep — the mighty ocean. The usual service was read, and the corpse, with a fearful plunge, sank into the sea, there to rest till the archangel's trump shall awake the sleeping millions and call them to judgment.

17th. — Passengers are disposed to put into Cape Town, and a petition has been drawn up and presented to the captain with this request, at least that it might be done for provisions and water, as we are again placed on a quart allowance, and that so slimy it is scarcely endurable. We have food of no description sufficient to last the voyage through, especially at present rates of sailing; for we have already been from Bahia long enough to have reached Australia under ordinary circumstances.

Many felt like saying, "We must and will go to Cape Town, and are prepared, if necessary, to rise and take the ship, and carry it through ourselves." The captain objects for no apparent reason but to indulge his capricious and reckless temper.

How can we expect any thing but ruin with such a captain, an insubordinate crew, and all the dangers which rum can possibly cause, staring us in the face?

22d. — At eleven, A. M., the joyful cry of "land" was again heard. It was Table Mountain, the three distinct summits of which are visible in clear weather at a distance of forty miles. The heavy fog only permitted us an occasional glimpse, though we were much nearer than this; yet it was sufficient to cause much excitement. While beating about, a small coasting sloop hailed us, with the information that we were nearing an extensive reef, and, of course, in new and close proximity to danger. After considerable solicitation, the captain was prevailed upon to take one of her men on board as pilot, though it was a sullen consent. Left to ourselves we should have probably been dashed to pieces in one half hour more, on the horn of a reef across which our course would have taken us. As it was, we quickly made the mouth of the harbor, or rather roadstead, for Cape Town is one of the most dangerous places for anchorage, called a harbor, in the whole world. Not being safe to run in this evening we shall lay off until morning, eagerly wishing for the wasting of the lagging hours.

23d. — A most magnificent and striking appearance was visible in the heavens last night,

TABLE BAY

upon which we gazed with intense interest —
a species of lunar bow. The sky was full of
small, detached clouds of a threatening and
watery aspect. The moon herself was not
visible, her place being known only as the
center of a circular area of colored light. This
was bounded by a large and broad ring of rich
and strongly-defined prismatic colors, the space
within which was filled with an indescribably
gorgeous display of mingled and endlessly-
shifting masses of the same color, varying and
blending like the forms in a gigantic kaleido-
scope, yet with a steady motion, instead of the
precipitate changes of that instrument. Even
far without the ring, the sullen faces of the
clouds were flecked and tinged with the same
bright hues.

There were evidently two distinct strata of
these "*cirri*," and they were racing in opposite
directions. The partial openings and inter-
lacings of these two across the broad, pale disk
of light in the moon's place, formed a strange
and startling play, taking to themselves various intricate combinations, like the wheels
within wheels one sometimes sees in brilliant

fireworks. It was altogether a rich and rare spectacle.

This morning we had a heavy gale and high sea, making it dangerous to be in the harbor, though anchored. We were utterly weary with the sea, and were all desirous of running in, even at the risk of our lives, hoping we might be fortunate enough to plant our feet once more upon land. The pilot, a weather-beaten old Dutchman, thought it a matter of doubt if we were able to land, but if we said so, he would try. We said so—he put her before the wind, and at a terrific rate we surged along upon the immense seas, under close-reefed topsails, passed the long line of breakers by the Lion's Rump, and dropped anchor abreast of the town. In less than two hours the custom-house officers and the consul, George S. Holmes, Esq., came on board in a boat. We were told we had performed a most presumptuous and hazardous experiment; that we had been watched from Telegraph Hill, with the most intense anxiety, in the momentary expectation that we should be swamped, or dashed to pieces upon the rocks. In a little time, notwithstanding the heavy sea, a majority of the passengers went on shore, — preferring the dangerous risk of landing, and a bath in the surf, rather than to wait on board a day or two longer. On landing, our eyes were greeted with the sight of a familiar thing — the schooner Euphrasia, of New York, bound for Australia, which we had left at Bahia, but was now in the harbor before us.

29th. — Our first inclination upon landing at Cape Town was to ramble about the place, and feast our eyes with such land luxuries as we could find. We found the town to be regularly laid out, containing several good squares; broad and straight streets, crossing each other at right angles, many of them watered by canals, planted on either side with trees, in the Dutch fashion. The houses are mostly built of brick or granite, flat-roofed, and chiefly white, with green windows; being large and airy, with an elevated terrace in front, and small gardens in the rear. British residents in India frequently resort hither for their health; so the town has generally the appearance of bustle and gayety. The environs are picturesque, and many beautiful gardens, laid out between it and the surrounding mountains, add very much to the pleasing effect.

The population is said to be thirty thousand, made up, as we thought, of every conceivable nation on earth; for we were not long in discovering Dutch, Hottentots, Malays, Abyssinians, Chinese, and English. We also noticed liveried persons, hanging on to the back of elegant carriages, and coachmen in the same garb of servitude; so there is evidently aristocracy in Cape Town.

The pronunciation of this place, as I learned it at school, I find to be erroneous, the people here pronouncing it as a word of two syllables, with the accent on the first instead of the last, as we are accustomed to make it. It looks out west and north upon the open sea, from a level plain between the shore and Table Mountain, which stretches behind it, and continues south and west in an irregular curve, until it ends at the southern point of the bay, in the disjointed, rounded summit, called the Lion's Rump. The town has a pervadingly English aspect,

ARISTOCRACY CAPE TOWN.

though very much modified by the people and
accessories of the numerous other races that
inhabit it. Being a military station, its streets
seem, to us Americans, literally to swarm with
officers and sentinels on duty.

Of the ten thousand slender, swarthy Malays,
some few are intelligent and wealthy; most,
however, are an exceedingly stupid set, retaining all their slothful orientalisms, and taking
no thought for the morrow. They, as well as
the Hottentots, and other races not of European blood, generally called "coolies," are
governed by a special class of enactments,
copies of which are posted conspicuously over
the town, on large sign-boards, six feet square,
like the rates on a toll bridge or turnpike gate;
prescribing their wages, hours of daily labor,
weight of burdens to be carried, &c. Any one
desirous of having a piece of work performed,
may call upon any of these not otherwise ac-
tively employed, and set them at work for the
legal time, at legal rates, and in case of refusal
they are imprisoned.

Our second day in town was spent mostly in
the Botanic Garden, really a "scientific para-

dise," — if there is such a place, — perhaps unequaled in interest by any of its size in the world. It covers an area of twenty acres, on one side of the magnificent avenue, so called, and directly opposite the stately Government House, the official residence of the governor of Cape Colony. The garden is in bloom the year round; and coming in the middle of it we find the camellias (the size of thrifty peach trees) perfect masses of blossoms; the walks bordered with monthly roses, orange and lemon trees, filling the air with perfume; Cape jessamines, lilies, and innumerable varieties of geraniums, in full flower. If such is mid-winter, what must the splendor of summer be?

Our first Sabbath, we attended service at St. George's Cathedral, which stands within the gate of the avenue, adjoining the grounds of the Government House. The music was, perhaps, the most impressive part of the service to us, the chanting being performed by a choir of boys, with sweet and well-trained voices. The sacred quiet of the place, together with the delicious music, deeply affected our hearts, and awakened within us many thoughts and feelings which had become torpid, in the foul and unwholesome atmosphere of our godless ship. Souls, like steel, rust under certain corroding circumstances.

Good fortune, I find, has not wholly forsaken me. Through the influence of one of our shipmates I have formed a pleasant and profitable acquaintance with a young English officer but lately returned from an expedition, with his regiment, into the Kaffir country. Being one of two or three invited to his home, we found it a cottage, three miles from the town, on the Wynberg road, literally covered with roses, geraniums, and jessamines; situated upon a small eminence, overlooking the town and the limitless Atlantic beyond. His pretty young wife and children met us at the door, and welcomed us cordially to the hospitalities of their home. After a luxurious dinner we related to him the story of our sufferings and hairbreadth escapes, receiving in return narratives of adventures in the field, for ours upon the flood. A bunch of assegais and arrows, tipped with virulent poison, a stout Kaffir bow, a war club with a round head, set with sharp knobs, like the old German "morgenstern," hung upon the wall.

Sitting beneath these pagan trophies, he displayed to us the complete suit of stout leather in which he made the campaign against the Kaffirs, and told us the occurrences of the war, in which we were much interested. The troops had notice at one time, it seems, of a body of Kaffirs concealed in the depths of a vast forest, and immediately marched against them.

Advancing as far as possible with horses, they left them guarded, and went forward through the dense "chapparal," as they call it, having borrowed a word from Mexico, seemingly, to serve their purpose. The low trees and underbrush becoming at last too thick to be penetrated, they actually scrambled a mile or two over their tops, as we had done through the masses of undergrowth in the forests of Brazil, came by surprise upon the enemy, and routed them with considerable loss. It is generally found, however, to be useless to operate against these hardy and athletic foemen with any thing less rapid and efficient than cavalry.

An invitation to protract our stay as we chose was gladly accepted, and the next morning found us on an excursion before breakfast, in company with our host. The first thing that attracted our attention was the huge wagons of the Cape, the dimensions of which may be imagined by the size of the largest wheels, which are sometimes ten feet high, with a hub like a hogshead, and an enormous iron tire a foot in width. These gigantic vehicles are drawn by twelve, twenty, and even thirty cattle, guided by two or three men, who make long journeys to and from the country with produce, finding particular convenience in their wide wheels, which enable them to pass over the loose, shifting sands, which they sometimes find on their return, in hills of ten feet, where they had before found a hard and level road.

The oxen are longer limbed than ours, with narrow, wild-looking faces, and immense horns bending upwards and outwards with a parabolic curve; sometimes five and six feet in length, and spreading so as to measure more than ten feet.

After an hour or two of rambling we returned to breakfast. These pleasant social meals at table are a wonderful luxury to us, after our long condemnation to the vulgar method of carrying our food to a corner to eat. We sat a long time enjoying it, though we had in prospect an excursion to Table Mountain, reckoned a good day's jaunt. We started rather late, and strolled leisurely up the slopes toward the mountain, passing ponds overgrown with calla Æthiopia, as thick and weed-like as pond lilies at home.

As we passed through a grove of African pine we met two seafaring men, rambling about like ourselves, in one of whom, to my surprise, I recognized Captain McDowell, of the schooner Euphrasia. We had a long interview, conversing upon various matters, during which he informed me of his intention to open business in Australia, having a full, assorted cargo of goods, groceries, and liquors for that purpose, and concluded by offering to furnish me a stock of merchandise on excellent terms, if I wished to enlist in that direction. But finding that the sale of the "fiery element" would be a necessary department of the business, I declined the undertaking.

Only two of the company ascended the mountain, as it began to grow foggy, and the precipitous and rugged character of it render it exceedingly dangerous at such times, beside shutting out the prospect.

They wandered about till they found themselves in the "table cloth," a heavy, dense fog, which often envelops the summit. They had discretion, however, to follow the rules for such cases; sat quietly down, and remained folded in their cool blanket through the night, and returned in the morning chilled, weary, and hungry; glad to escape the fate of one who had some time before been dashed to pieces upon the rugged rocks below, by attempting to find his way down.

Wynberg road is a favorite walk with us, being the most perfect I have ever seen — built in the thorough, macadamized manner of the English — well-graded, even, smooth, hard, with very little dust, and a surface almost inky black.

It is lined on both sides, a distance of almost

eight miles, with cottages and country seats, gardens, vineyards, and parks, all very neatly kept and in high cultivation.

In the Wynberg prison is confined Seyolo, the Kaffir chief, long the most powerful ruler in that part of Africa, and the worst enemy of the English colony. About five months since, he voluntarily surrendered himself to government, and has since been kept in confinement. Gaining permission to visit him, we entered his cell, when he arose, extended his hand, and gave us a cordial greeting. He appears about twenty-seven years of age, being six feet and one inch in height, and of the most perfect proportions. His skin is quite dark, his head well-formed and high, his eye full, mild, and expressive; his mouth really beautiful, and his teeth of pure whiteness. Altogether, his countenance expresses fine and manly feelings, and much intelligence; not any thing of the savage nature and habits we had expected to read in it.

He has several wives, one of whom is with him — a shy little creature of sixteen, with a beautiful hand and full, dark eyes. She gazed upon us a moment, and then coiling herself, like a serpent, in her blanket, remained out of sight, silent and motionless, until we departed.

Various are the places we have visited, and the excursions we have made, while with this pleasant family; but such detentions are not what we desire, provided we could have tolerable arrangements in a direct voyage to Australia — the place of our destination.

July 4th was ushered in by a glorious anniversary sunrise. Although in a foreign port, and a military station, the Americans and lovers of liberty were wide awake for a celebration. The port regulations would not permit a salute to be fired; consequently their enthusiasm was spent in a dinner, spiced with music, speeches, &c.

We had intended to sail this afternoon; indeed, we were ready to sail four days after entering this port, and should have done so, but the French passengers lodged a protest against the captain, with the consul, charging him with trying to run the ship ashore twice, as well as several other violations of duty. Upon this he was imprisoned, and was only liberated by the intervention of passengers who desired to be on their way, and not from any good will to him.

He is determined to revenge, in some way or other; and of course it is an obstacle to our progress.

10th. — We were, through much difficulty, able to go out to sea on the 5th. The seas, in this part of the ocean, are the heaviest in the world; and within a few moments there will arise around us such billows as I never dreamed of before. At seven, last evening, the wind began to rise, the clouds to wear a lurid aspect, which was soon followed by rolling thunder and flashing lightning. The vessel was thrown upon her beam ends, and a leak forced its way through; but this was soon remedied, and we are still alive, through the infinite mercy of Him who rules the winds and waves.

17th. — We have passed through a storm fearful indeed. The heavens grew dark, filled with clouds like the lurid masses from which the first heavy burst of rain sometimes falls in our summer thunder storms at home, but beyond measure more vast and threatening in aspect, and rapid in movement. It appeared as if each were a reservoir of a hideous tempest, discharging their streams upon us, and the water about us, with such power as to send us careering upon the bounding waves in utter confusion. I saw repeatedly two of these precipitous waves sweeping toward us at once, curling high above our low bulwarks from opposite sides, apparently ready to break upon our heads, when we would slide beyond them, or rise nearly to their summit upon some third billow, that lifted us from below like some gigantic hand.

Sometimes, from the top of a mountain wave, I could look for miles over the vast ocean desert, and the next moment would find us buried in the depths beneath.

Night closed around us, and the storm abated not in the least. The black heavens were above us, and the angry seas beneath, while around us on every side swept the furious wind. The situation of two hundred souls, — men, women, and children, — shut up in a little space below, thrown helplessly hither and thither for so many desperate hours, was painful in the extreme.

While endeavoring to administer some comfort to some of the feebler victims, I heard a crash on deck, followed by the sound of rushing water through the thick planking on deck. Repairing to the spot, I found the jib-boom and fore-topmast had been carried away, the former gone overboard; the latter, tangled with rigging and shattered spars, lay across the bulwarks. The captain appeared with a face whiter than I ever supposed his red visage could ever be, and exclaimed, "O God, all is lost!"

He ordered the main spencer to be set, and went into the cabin, making an effort to condole with the passengers, the extremity of the danger having, for once, made him really human. Our condition was now known to all, and the scene in the crowded cabin was solemn indeed; for the expectation was universal that the gigantic seas would soon finish what the wind had begun. A short consultation among those who held the sustaining hopes of the gospel, and were therefore free from the abject fears and lamentations of others, resulted in a decision to hold a meeting for prayer in our extremity. The suggestion was eagerly received, and an Englishman named Croke, a local Methodist preacher, together with Buckley and myself, conducted a service brief and simple, but earnest enough, being made impressive by its dreadful reality.

We reminded the groaning and weeping company of their loose, ungodly lives, and great wickedness, even on this voyage, and urged the duty of immediate repentance, and looking to God for mercy.

It was also said, — and it was my own firm belief, — that we had not been brought so far on our way, through such imminent perils, to be destroyed now.

We reminded them of the two escapes from shipwreck on the coast; of the third on the South African reef; the fourth, in entering Table Bay; the fifth, in the calm after we had left it; of our providential supplies of water north of the line; of the still more wonderful salvation from death by fire; and by thus presenting the hopes which animated us, we calmed, in some measure, the general fright.

The captain himself summoned all hands to a second meeting of the same kind afterward, and was one of the most attentive hearers. The evening witnessed a third no less earnest and serious. The homely prayers and ill-sung psalms could not but have a solemn meaning, when the starving, drenched, weary, and dispirited congregation were thrown every moment hither and thither by the tempests of Him whom they addressed — when they asked preservation from danger against which human effort was utterly powerless — which threatened to bury them speedily in the depths of the sea. The women wept quietly; the men prayed and groaned, and even the weather-beaten face of our wicked old commander was wet with unaccustomed tears.

At the close of the service the hurricane was still at its height, and the same enormous seas still breaking over our dismantled ship. At midnight, however, there was a sudden change. The clouds were dissipated and scattered; the wind and the sea fell with a strange rapidity, the whole appearing no less than a signal answer to prayer, which called forth a service of thanksgiving this morning — the first Sabbath observance among the ship's company for nearly six months.

20th. — Various expedients have been resorted to, for the purpose of repairing the damage done to the ship; but most of the experiments prove insufficient as yet. By means of a floating spar, we are heading toward the Isle of France — have made about fifty miles.

24th. — Fine weather. The captain himself made arrangements for "church service," and tolled the bell as the summons to divine worship. Croke gave us a short and sensible discourse, from Rev. xxii. 1 and 2 verses.

The dangers so recently escaped, our present disabled condition on a vessel little better than a wreck, the unknown perils to be met before we reach our anticipated port, the chances that we never reach it, or any other, are ample reasons for seriousness in our audience. Yet I cannot avoid the painful conviction that most of them are frightened into solemnity for the time being.

28th. — Surely no one ever penned a truer line, than that "joy and sorrow meet together." It is verily so, we thought, as a thrill of joy went through every heart, at the cry of "land," this morning, and almost a moment after saw the assembled company on deck witnessing themselves slowly drifting toward the shore of Madagascar, upon a heavy swell.

The captain ordered another effort to be made to get the first jury rudder into efficient operation. After an hour or two of cutting, carving, and hoisting, the attempt succeeded, amid tears and cheers of the whole ship's company. Through the day, however, we gradually approached the land, and at evening could plainly see the rugged outlines and green forests of the hills near the coast, and the successive ranges that rose one behind another toward the interior.

A light breeze, springing up, has carried us

out to sea again, saving us, in all human probability, not only from shipwreck, but from the weapons and teeth of the cannibals who inhabit this part of the coast.

August 5th. — This monotony and suspense, together with the scarcity of water and provisions, are producing an unfavorable effect upon many minds and bodies. Nervous complaints are becoming frequent among men, women, and children. Moreover, we have detected the terrible signs of scurvy, but have agreed to keep this startling news to ourselves, at least for the present, confining our efforts to the maintenance of good spirits, and some degree of healthful activity among our sickly and discouraged passengers.

6th. — A strange apathy and indifference has settled down upon nearly all. Our long series of disappointments and hardships has seemed to render hearts callous, and deaden the sensibilities of many. Nearly half are sick with a slow kind of ship fever, the result of general exhaustion from mental suffering and physical debility. Thin, yellow, haggard faces, wearing the most woe-begone looks, are plenty. Some neither wash nor go for their daily rations — one quart of water, the same quantity of rice, a little miserable bread, and salt junk. One poor fellow really set himself about dying. He has lain in his bunk, obstinately refusing to go on deck, or even move about for any purpose whatever. This excited considerable feeling, as, in the general unhealthiness, one such case might prove disastrous indeed. Having a brother-in-law of more cheerfulness than himself, who saw what was needed, he took a friend or two, and proceeded to the couch of Bob, saluting him in a strong and hopeful voice—"Halloa! What's all this? H'ist out there, Bob!" A groan accompanied the feeble answer, "I can't — I'm dying."

His visitors, considering that no unnecessary dying could be allowed on the ship, actually laid hands upon him, forced him upon deck, where they subjected him to a thorough bath, which he very much needed. Although the operation was any thing but agreeable, it has produced a favorable result, and he is now doing well. This day we sighted Bourbon, but with a head wind. The view, however, gives us a gleam of hope that we may succeed in reaching the Isle of France.

9th.—Yesterday we could discover trees and houses on the Bourbon Island, and the Picton de Nevis rising majestically above the other hills, furrowed throughout the whole ascent with many deep ravines and gorges, while here and there we could see small streams wandering down its sides. The sight really revived our spirits; but to-day we are blown off to sea again, and shall therefore have more difficulty in making the Isle of France. Our rudder chains have corroded rapidly upon the ship's copper, and have had to be successively replaced with such as could be spared from the rigging. Our last one from the main rigging has been put on, and in case of a heavy gale, our situation would be truly appalling. We can only trust in God.

CHAPTER VIII.

ENTER THE HARBOR OF PORT LOUIS. — VISIT AT THE ISLE OF FRANCE. — GRAVE OF HARRIET NEWELL. — A MALABAR FUNERAL. — ENTER THE BRIG NAUTILUS. — LAND AT MELBOURNE.

> "O, who can tell save he whose heart hath tried,
> And danced in triumph o'er the waters wide,
> The exulting sense — the pulse's maddening play —
> That thrills the wanderer of the trackless way."

Thus sang Byron; but methinks he would never have written of the "deep and dark-blue ocean" with as much serenity and enthusiasm had he been tossed upon the "bounding waste," in a miserable bark like ours, with the ever-recurring expectation of sinking in the depths, without a grave — "unknelled, uncoffined, and unknown."

The "triumph" and the "exultation" were more certainly ours on sight of land, when a near view of the much-wished-for isle greeted us on the 15th, as will be seen from this date.

Its whole outline is singular and striking, being broken with many jagged, pointed peaks, among which Peter Botte, with his straight shaft and high-capped summit, is king. The winter rains have left the island clothed in a mantle of fresh green.

To us half-starved, sea-worn wretches, the scene is as lovely as the Delectable Hills to Bunyan's poor pilgrims; and we gaze with profound delight upon the mountain tops; the misty clouds above them, and their sloping sides, dotted with plantations and villas, variegated with the bright colors of growing crops.

16th. — No sleep last night, for anxiety, hope, and fear. All hands were watching for the dawn; an incessant lookout being maintained for fear of reefs, as no one on board is acquainted with this part of the Indian Ocean. We were all night within a few miles of port, and at dawn, the breeze being very light and not favorable, we hoisted a signal of distress, and fired guns for any steamer that might be inside, this being one of the English mail stations.

In an hour or two a black steamship, from the Red Sea, came to our assistance, and towed us into the harbor of Port Louis, — a rusty, ragged, dirty set of us, — with our fair proportions sadly disfigured by the rickety little jury spars forward — an ungainly and woful spectacle.

A crowd, attracted by the sound of our guns, were gathered upon the mole to witness our arrival. The French, English, and American consuls came on board soon after we reached our anchorage, and more astonishment was never visible in human countenances than in theirs, as they beheld the wan faces and tat-. tered costumes of the passengers, the stripped and sea-beaten aspect of our shattered bulwarks and maimed spars, and the unheard-of number stowed away in our small quarters.

A brief examination drew from them the remark that we ought to be thankful to God that we had ever reached any port at all, in such a miserable condition. Their sympathies were so effectually excited, they offered to provide houses for our convenience and comfort on shore, each for his own nation. Some left the ship at once, but most of us have remained till sent for, being entirely destitute of money.

We are anchored near a Scotch vessel, which arrived two weeks before us, having been out in the same gale in which we lost our rudder. She was swept clean from stem to stern of bulwarks, deck houses, sails, and every thing except her bare spars, and the same time lost a passenger and sailor. She too is bound for Australia, and is in for repairs.

All day we have received visits from the citizens of the place, and from neighboring vessels. Many friendly people, hearing of our destitution, have brought and distributed among us quantities of delicious fruit — a most welcome gift.

Early in the evening, some, desirous of enjoying themselves at every possible opportunity, commenced an entertainment of vocal and instrumental music; and with songs, speeches, and cheering, the moonlight jubilee has lasted long. It is almost like a transition from purgatory to paradise. The dreary experiences of the past are forgotten; and so, alas! is the hand of God who brought us through them. Once safe in port, and sure of going ashore to-morrow, nothing is heard or remembered of prayers or thanksgivings. Such is man's ingratitude.

25th. — Early on the 17th, the captain came with two scows, one for us and another for our baggage. In a few moments we were landed upon the stone steps leading into the custom house. Here our beggarly chattels were drawn up and submitted to the inspection of the government officials, who lumped them all together as a parcel of trash, not worth imposing a duty on. Poor as they were, they were, nevertheless, indispensable to us; and securing them as best we could, we marched through the heart of the crowded and curious city to our allotted abodes, presenting an appearance, it must be acknowledged, somewhat like prison birds, with our negligent sea clothes, and despairing expressions, induced by our long train of suffering, and graven so deeply as not to be effaced by even twenty hours of physical comfort and safety.

Indeed, reflection brought but little gladness, for most of us were absolutely penniless, having spent all our funds in outfit, passage money, subscribing to pay the ship's bills, or current expenses.

We were directed to a large stone storehouse, one hundred and twenty-five feet in length, nearly full of goods, with an airy garret, loosely floored, which was to be our home for a little time. We at once "located" upon separate portions of the floor, arranged our small property, and commenced housekeeping in good earnest. Fresh provisions and fruit were served out to us every morning, and each mess cooked in turn, having but one place for the operation. We luxuriated in the unbounded supply of fresh water, and lost no time in effecting thorough purification of our persons and clothing, realizing the truth of Thomson's sentiment, that —

> "Even from the body's purity the mind
> Receives a secret, sympathetic aid."

Thus being rendered little more human, by Nature's own element, we turned our attention to things about us, and to the history of the place.

Port Louis, it seems, was originally settled by the French, and most of its buildings are in a French style, but now mainly occupied by the English; although the population, numbering about twenty thousand, includes representatives from at least eighteen different nations. It is almost encircled by a range of mountains, which, with the sea, enclose as delightful a garden as can be found on earth, filled with all the luxury and magnificence of the tropics.

The city contains many fine buildings, has wide, handsome streets, with gas, abundance of water, and is a busy commercial place.

The real founder of this important settlement was the justly celebrated M. de la Bourdonnaye, who was made governor in 1734. Perceiving the importance of the island, which its two excellent harbors rendered of the greatest consequence to any European power having, or wishing to have, possessions in India, he set about its improvement with a zeal, sagacity, and success, that have rarely been equaled, never surpassed.

He constructed numerous roads, aqueducts, and other public works, and fixed the seat of government here, which he may be said to have created as well as fortified. For the space of eleven years only his administration continued; but it was sufficient for him to change the whole aspect of the country, and render it a prosperous and valuable colony.

Sad though it seem, these signal services met with a most ungrateful return. On his return to France, in 1748, he was thrown into the Bastile, where he was immured more than three years, and as the sequel proved, without the smallest foundation for any of the charges made against him. He died the victim of this disgraceful treatment in 1755.

This island, it is well known, is the scene of St. Pierre's inimitable tale of Paul and Virginia. The wreck of the St. Geran, so striking and affecting an incident in the story, is a real event, which took place on the 18th of August, 1744.

The whole island is full of delightful scenery. The climate is faultless, and it is already a place of considerable resort for invalids. When steam navigation shall become more general, the place will, undoubtedly, become a strong attraction to thousands of health seekers, as well as those in pursuit of pleasure. At present there is only the arrival of the monthly English mail steamer from Suez, and departures for Calcutta and Australia.

We noticed in the auction marts numbers of Arabian merchants; the noblest specimens of physical development I have ever seen — stately, dignified, and well proportioned, with noble faces, olive complexions, large black eyes, and magnificent beards. Some of them were mounted on beautiful Arab horses, and others made use of carriages of English manufacture. One of the most attractive spots in the neighborhood is the cemetery, on the sea shore, about a mile and a half from the city, where many travelers, health-seeking invalids, and missionaries have been buried; among whom is Mrs. Harriet Newell, who reposes in a spot lovely enough for the last resting place even of one as heavenly as she.

In striking contrast with this Christian burial, as I imagined it, was a Malabar funeral,

GRAVE OF HARRIET NEWELL,
ISLE OF FRANCE.

which came under my observation in the immediate vicinity. The corpse was carried in a crescent-shaped car, ten feet in length, made of reeds and light wicker, and gayly decorated with bits of ribbon, flowers, brass ornaments, bells, and any thing whatever, to make a show and a noise.

This was supported by four men, before whom went a procession of natives, dancing, sparring, shouting, and blowing horns till they arrived at the grave, when the corpse was fed with a mixture of rice and sand, and some pennies given it to pay its passage to heaven. They ended their ceremony by the washing of hands in a pond in the cemetery, smoking a funeral pipe together on a grass plat, and dividing the effects of the deceased, which by their custom are distributed among the whole circle of friends. Alas for these deluded victims of a miserable superstition! How much they need the civilizing and enlightening influences of a holier religion!

The Malabar women wear all manner of ornaments in their ears and nostrils, and on their arms and ankles; some of them having considerable capital thus invested, and look like walking jewelry shops.

During my stay on the island, I have made several new acquaintances; some by chance, and some by means of a flat-iron. When first settled in our attic, we did a great business in washing and smoothing our clothes; and as the above instrument was owned by my friend, John Harman, he became as much of a benefactor and favorite by lending it to one and another, both men and women, as if he could have "touched" successfully "for the king's evil." Its fame spread even beyond the precincts, for it seemed it was almost unheard-of on the island. By loaning it to one family and another he secured the most flattering invitations for himself and a friend or two to dinner and tea, in many of which I participated. The inestimable treasure has, I believe, been finally presented to some favored damsel.

From a merchant, with whom I have become acquainted, I have received an offer of employment upon favorable terms, and with good prospects for the future; but the spirit of wandering is upon me, and I decline. Already I am tired of delaying upon the Isle of France, and am anxiously looking for an opportunity to pursue the voyage to Australia.

26th. — My anticipations are realized, and that in the most unexpected manner. Mr. Werihe, of the house of Francis and Co., on the island, is found to be a relative of Clark, and the knowledge has called forth his sympathy and benevolence on our behalf. He offers to pay for the passage to Australia for two or three of us, and we gladly accept the offer, and shall therefore leave forever our ship Peytona, and embark on the brig Nautilus, Captain Scott, of two hundred tuns, bound for Melbourne with a cargo of sugar.

28th. — Once more on the waters. We did not look at our accommodations in advance, considering the trip as merely the fulfillment of our "manifest destiny;" and it may not be surprising, perhaps, that we find it a rickety, dilapidated "sugar box," filled to its utmost capacity. Twenty-four of us are stowed in the hold, where a room has been arranged, walled up to the deck with bags of sugar and casks of liquor cases, having no entrance except through the main hatch. Here we are to sit all day, if we choose, and lie all night, having particularly *sweet* rest, if the material of the bed has any thing to do with it.

We are to cook for ourselves, taking turns with the little Creole boy, who is waiter, steward, and cabin boy, for captain and officers, beside being cook for the vessel's crew.

September 18th. — It is generally agreed by us, that this voyage is more dangerous, if possible, than that on the Peytona; perhaps a trifle less disagreeable. We have, thus far, had a succession of gales, that have kept us nearly all the time under double-reefed and close-reefed top-sails, and, together with our cramped and comfortless situation, have quite put an end to my writing for a time.

Drunkenness is the order of things here also. The captain, suspecting the sailors of furnishing themselves from the wrong source, held an investigation of the matter, whereupon the "dumb mouths" of his empty bottles told a conclusive story. Upon this he summoned all hands upon the quarter-deck, read to the culprits the severe provisions of the English law relative to stealing on shipboard, and briefly proposed the alternative of settling the matter by paying for the missing brandy at retail rates, or awaiting the course of the law.

Upon consultation they paid the amount demanded; but these seamen are a jovial, shrewd company — constantly leaguing together in the accomplishment of some act of roguery. They know enough to avoid dissension among themselves; are friendly and helpful; have plenty of money, and abound beyond measure in songs and anecdotes, with which they beguile many an idle hour. The Englishman with us is one of those who was continually irritating our national pride on the Peytona with the most odious kind of comparisons; constantly referring to the superior accommodations, provisions, and regulations on "Henglish vessels;" daily vexing our hearts with remarks upon the innumerable evils of our lot, as if they were not sufficient of themselves, without being magnified.

But here we are on an English vessel. We had no very definite expectations, perhaps, but certainly some indistinct ideas of good treatment and decent food; but our "grub" on the Peytona was really almost "first-class-hotel" fare, compared with this. Our bread is the worst sort of "English tile," that might be worked into boiler plates for hardness. The worst of the Peytona's beef, ill-smelling as it was, and requiring diligent and faithful mastication, could yet be eaten; but here it is soft and sickening, from miserable putrefaction.

Our tea, as the seamen say,— and they are competent judges,— is not a Chinese, but an Australian product; a bogus article, manufactured from the leaves of some of the fragrant shrubs there, and the taste is such as to convince me of the truth of the story.

Our water is kept in a large iron tank, and is as yellow as gold with iron-rust, besides being strongly impregnated with coal tar.

The mixture of pain and joy which Perrin, "the old man," extracts from this "bill of fare," is exceedingly comical. Holding up a soft lump of the putrefying substance, he exclaims with a doleful groan, "O dear, boys, have we got to eat such stuff as this?" "Yes," I reply; "no other way; down with it!" at the same time disposing of a piece of the same by the help of a morsel of bread, like a scrap of a cast-iron kettle, or next to it. With another look of utter misery, he turns with bitter irony to the unlucky Englishman, and continues, "O, no, this ain't bad beef! We're aboard an English vessel now, where they do things up in good style, serving out the best meat, and first-quality of bread, *always*. It's done accordin' to law."

Thus he torments the poor fellow, who is silent with shame, taking special delight in gratifying his revenge upon this reviler of American laws and customs.

These incessant taunts have driven him to the captain, to whom he has cited the text of the English statutes, frightening him into so much improvement that he has weighed out to us a comparatively fair week's allowance of endurable food. I have one secret source of consolation myself, which I take the liberty of keeping private; since discovery must necessarily deprive me of it.

It has availed to lighten somewhat the horrors of my individual lot; while my comrades innocently wonder at the patience with which I possess my soul, under our unjust treatment. This consolation is derived from a confidential and not wholly disinterested friendship, which I have managed to form with the over-worked little Creole cook. He is wanted all day long in, at least, two places at once, and finds a hard time in running of errands for the officers, cooking for passengers, and preparing the viands of the cabin mess in a manner satisfactory to the palates of the commander and his mates.

I have installed myself as "cook-substitute" to this young dignitary, and while watching the savory messes of meats, vegetables, &c., I abstract now and then some "unconsidered trifle," which, of course, is only wages for work done, but an unspeakable comfort to me.

October 3d. — Gales and cold weather have been the characteristics of our voyage. Yesterday, at 8 A. M., we made Cape Otway, and at 7 P. M. saw the lighthouse at the Heads. This morning we passed between the bold and lofty points called the Heads of Port Philip Bay, and are now anchored at its upper extremity, opposite Sandridge, a miserable village near the shore, two miles from Melbourne by a direct road through swamps and heavy sands. It is nine miles to the city by the River Yarra Yarra, on which it is situated, and which sweeps around in a semicircle, from the city to the bay. Many ships are constantly arriving and departing to and from all parts of the world. Nearly a thousand sail are now anchored in the bay.

4th. — This morning no breakfast was served out to us; the ship having brought us to Melbourne, according to the spirit of the nautical contract, and owed us a living no longer. We took the hint, paid a boatman one pound to put us ashore — a true-gold-country price for a few rods of boating; but we did not grudge it, although it took almost our last farthing to place our feet on land once more. We packed our portable property, hired a dray for the heavy baggage, to transport us to the borders of Canvas-town, a distance of two miles, where poor or transient persons are permitted to erect tents on a piece of land belonging to government, for small rents.

We have arrived just at the close of the rainy season, and find the weather exceedingly unpleasant. We have erected a temporary shelter, on sloping ground, close under the wall of the Park, having no fuel but such as we can pick up about us. We have bought a little flour and a little mutton, purposing only to stay until we can obtain direct and reliable information concerning mining operations, which we are anxious to commence.

CHAPTER IX.

STAY AT CANVAS-TOWN. — JOURNEY TO BALLERAT. — PURCHASE OF A CLAIM. — EXPERIENCE IN THE MINES. — DISAPPOINTMENT OF THE WARDY-ALLOCK EXPEDITION. — RETURN TO BALLERAT.

25th. — Having spent about two weeks in Canvas-town gaining information from different individuals, which was a contradictory mass of advice, as might be supposed, and having disposed of nearly all our scanty jewelry and hardware in the purchase of provisions, we decided to proceed to Ballerat, as being the deepest and richest mines, and therefore likely to afford us the more abundant remuneration. I sold my watch for seven pounds, and, with one or two trifling additions which we succeeded in raising, we obtained the needed outfit for miners, and had a few dollars remaining.

We left our place of abode early in the

morning, taking care that no one should be acquainted with our intention before the time, as we had often seen the tax-gathering gentry pacing up and down for the revenues of the British crown, and our lank purses feared their visits.

Ballerat is about a hundred miles from Melbourne, west of north; and Geelong, on an arm of the bay, forty miles; but the road from the latter being much the best, and the usual route to the "diggings," we decided to take it, and embarked on a steamer, which we found to be none other than the identical Duncan Hoyle, which we had spoken seven months before while crossing the line, in the Atlantic, and whose half-wrecked appearance had created some solicitude in the minds of many. She had been dismantled and refitted, and was now plying regularly between Melbourne and Geelong.

Upon arriving at the latter place, no drays were ready, and we prepared to encamp outside the town on the wet ground. A Scotch family, whose residence was but a few rods distant, sent us some hot tea, and an invitation to spend the night with them, which we accepted most thankfully. Here we had a sumptuous repast of various savory viands, especially those pleasant, fragile cakes, which an old friend of mine in New England, significantly, if not sanctimoniously, calls "Vanity."

Our host was young, intelligent, full of spirit and good nature, and evidently enjoyed life with a keen zest. He had made considerable money in "smuggling," under the absurd English system of high duties and a protective force, but, a year or two before our visit, had been detected, imprisoned, tried, and condemned; paid his fine of two thousand pounds, and was living comfortably on the remainder.

We joined ourselves to a party of fifteen Americans, or, as the English call every body from Anglo-Saxon America, "Yankees," who had overtaken us on their way to the mines. Two of the men were accompanied by their wives, Boston girls, one not twenty years of age, who were too spirited to let their husbands go even to Australia without them.

Being disappointed in finding conveyances,

as they had expected, they resolutely prepared to walk. Two drays, whose drivers were acquainted with the route, and could serve as guides, were employed to transport the provisions and baggage of the party. The first day we traveled eighteen miles over hills and through valleys, in mud and water for miles together. The ladies endured the fatigue wonderfully, although one of them had her feet so blistered as to make it doubtful whether she could proceed. We camped on the brow of a high hill, on a spot of dry ground, and thought ourselves too much exhausted to eat. After a little rest, however, we made a large fire, boiled our tea, and cooked our mutton, and with dry bread made a meal that would have satisfied an epicure, — if he had done our day's work.

Clark, who seemed to think that in Australia there must needs be gold in every stream, would not be dissuaded from surveying the wet valley below. With shovel in hand, he repaired to the bank of a small river, and spent an hour in the mud, with as much chance of success as he would have had in a bushel of Connecticut clay, and came up again to find himself the subject of ridicule.

At sunset the next day we were twenty-five miles further on our way, having come through open Australian forests, many trees of which were covered with blossoms, and vocal with the everlasting chatter of numerous parrots of a variety of colors. We saw also several of the beautiful "birds of paradise" and mocking birds.

No man can ever know the perfect relish of food and drink, or the perfect sweetness of sleep, until he takes them after a day's weary walking, in the open air, by the light and warmth of the blazing camp-fire.

Toward the close of our journey we met several returning from the mines. The invariable greeting here is, "Well! mate!" and a chat commences at once, by an exchange of data as to destination, starting place, &c. Those who have been unfortunate speak discouragingly of matters in the mines; others give a glowing account, and are strong in the assurance one may be rich if he will — a statement pleasant to believe, by those walking in the vale of poverty.

We entered the "city of Ballerat" through a valley running northward between two hills, called "Yankee Gully," which opens out into a comparatively level space, called the "Flat." This and the hills around are dotted with the homes of miners. We came to Ballerat for the very reason the mines were the deepest; but on the very first sight of the shafts, into which we looked with anxious curiosity, we felt it to be a most discouraging spectacle. Some of the pits are a hundred and fifty feet deep, stretching down into impenetrable darkness. A clumsy wooden frame carries an axle and two cranks, at which a couple of weary, forbidding-looking creatures slowly turn to raise the bucket of earth, water, or mud from which they hope to extract the shining particles which will compensate for their hard labor. Meanwhile their comrades are at work by lamplight below.

"Have we got to work in such places?" groaned Perrin, with a most disconsolate look. "Why, how did you suppose it was done?" I inquired. "Well, by sorting over the gravel, and picking out the lumps of gold." So far from such a prospect, I think it will be realizing the truth of the old proverb to its fullest extent — " Whosoever will find gold must *dig*."

28th. — There are said to be about twenty thousand souls in this place or about it, all striving and hoping to amass a handsome pile of the golden ore.

Our first object was to proceed to the camp of the English commissioner for license, having been informed that the regulations were very severe; so much so, that any one remaining in Ballerat over a certain length of time, without a license, was liable to a heavy fine, imprisonment, or to be put to work on the public roads. We found him a middle aged, good-natured man, but not deficient in the inexorable rigidity seemingly requisite for an English official. To our statement that we had hardly sufficient in our pockets to provide food for our daily necessities, he listened civilly, and replied briefly, that any modification of the law was impossible. Finding that neither argument nor entreaty availed any thing, we promised ten dollars each for a printed license, which would give us permission to work fifteen days in one month, and the whole of another.

Having passed this disagreeable ordeal, the next thought was a *place of residence*. From the commissioner's camp ground we had a view of nearly all the Flat and the slopes around it. Below was the "city," a collection of white tents, over which were waving flags of various nations — the signs of the merchants in many instances. These are displayed upon tall poles, and make a brilliant display, some of them being quite magnificent in proportion and design.

We were surprised to see the "stars and stripes" outnumbering the banners of any other nation; indeed, Ballerat may almost be called an American settlement, so numerous are the Yankees. We have decided to encamp somewhere in the suburbs, rather than in the business neighborhood, and accordingly turned our attention to the brow of Black Hill, where the trees offer their grateful shade, and the crest of the hill will defend us from the wind, at least in one quarter.

29th. — We have planted ourselves, unmolested, upon the proposed spot; have stretched a tent-pole between two trees, thrown a cloth over it, and deposited within our scanty chattels, thus establishing ourselves in house-keeping in our own private mansion. Finding *advice* from miners of little account, we determined to proceed to operations in our own way. Clark and Perrin were bent upon sinking a shaft near our tent; but, thinking them foolish, I shouldered my tools and went to the top of the hill, known as "Ballerat Bank," as an industrious miner is almost always sure of moderate wages from its vault of dust. Things I must confess, appear rather dubious, for it seems like working only to be tantalized with the sight of immovable rock, that has stood, strata underlying strata, since the world began, and with a fair prospect of remaining till the end of time, despite the efforts of puny man, who would fain turn them over to see if gold lies at the bottom.

November 5th. — Having labored upon the hill two or three days with no success, I abandoned the project as hopeless, and turned to a deserted pit at some distance. Around the sides and bottom of this I did better, being able, at the close of the first day, to show several dollars of the dull-yellow grains, which I had extracted from earth almost as hard as stone. Upon this my two partners deserted their shaft, now about twenty feet deep, and entered the cave with me; where we made fair wages, accumulating several ounces in a little time. Some Yankees from below, hearing of our success, and supposing we were among the "lucky ones," bound to succeed, invited us to come among the aristocracy of the Flat; that is, those who had sufficient capital to enable them to sink a shaft.

Being somewhat elated by our recent gains, we yielded to their solicitations, and organized a party, staking out a claim of legal dimensions, — twelve feet square, — among the diggings on Ballerat Flat.

The gold lies in a very crooked gutter, apparently the bed of an ancient stream, from fifty to a hundred feet below the present level. Thus, by a vast expenditure of labor, as uncertain of reward as a lottery, the course of the gold has been traced upward until particles were no longer found grouped together, but scattered too thinly to pay for mining. The same has been done in the opposite direction. The gold is usually found in a thin stratum of gravel, below the white layer, called the "pipe clay," lying upon the living rock.

Some, in commencing the year with a fortune, have lost it before its close in sinking pits to no purpose. If a claim is successful, every inch of ground around it is instantly taken up, and a ring of shafts sunk, in the hope of obtaining vast quantities of the ore. As these go down, the jealous miners quarrel and fight over fancied encroachments, and the commissioner—the authority in all such cases—has to measure the precious earth over and over again. No one group of shafts can be carried down faster than another without draining them; and as most are too selfish to aid others, they have to proceed with about the same degree of rapidity. Probably not more than one shaft in four, certainly, pays any thing at all.

December 23d. — The life I have led for some time past being unfavorable to journalizing, I have dispensed with it altogether; and now, in a season of comparative quiet, I propose to review these past scenes and varied experiences.

The claim which we opened proving very wet, we gave it up after sinking it a few feet, and selected another in a dry spot, further down the valley. Having carried this down as far as practicable, without siding, we made an expedition into the woods for the purpose of obtaining material requisite for the purpose. This is necessary for the safety of the miners, as well as for excluding water. The Flat abounds in quicksands and singular subterranean collections of water, which often burst suddenly upon the workmen while under ground, and in spite of all their efforts at protection are almost certainly fatal. Many such accidents occurred to our knowledge, by one of which seven men lost their lives at once. Some of the bodies were never recovered, remaining buried near the treasures they had sought. Others rose to the surface of the blue-pit water, and were wrapped either in their tent cloth or bed clothes, and buried in the "Potter's Field," a place serving as a rude cemetery for the city.

The woods near Ballerat have been so thoroughly searched for suitable trees, that we traveled two miles before finding one. The gum trees, of which there are several varieties, are the principal timber trees of Australia. Almost all the trees of the country are traversed throughout their substance by irregular knots and veins of gum; most plentiful and troublesome, however, in the gum trees proper, which are sometimes so hard as almost to blunt iron instruments. When we had nearly completed our operations, Clark, our chief reliance in the mechanical department, struck an unlucky blow with his ax; the heavy blade glanced, and struck deep into his foot.

We bandaged it with handkerchiefs; formed a rough litter, and transported our unlucky mate to our tent on the brow of the hill; sent for a physician, who gave us very little consolation in saying that he would be laid aside, at least, three months. We could not prosecute our efforts further, as neither of us could fill his place, and we therefore concluded to retreat and make another attempt, as no time was to be lost. We went up and down the neighborhood, in wet places and in dry; sometimes in our old cavern in Ballerat Bank, and sometimes in old claims on the Flat.

I spent several profitable and exceedingly perilous days in Gold Hill, so called, where I descended some fifteen or twenty feet through an old shaft, and found myself amid darkness so profound that I could do nothing, till my eyes became accustomed to the fearful gloom. Then, with such a scanty light as I could strike up, I went creeping about, hither and thither, in the vast cavernous regions, sometimes twenty-five feet in hight, and again so low, one could only work his way with great difficulty. It has been gradually worked out above the gold-bearing strata, and is supported by earthy pillars, cut away to a size as slender as fear of instant death would allow. Here and there, as I dared I broke pieces from the portion of earth which formed the basis of these pillars, crushed them in my hands, extracting the precious grains as the rich reward of my courage.

While at work afterward in the yellow, muddy water of Ballerat Creek, washing the gravelly portion which the miners had washed before me, I fell in with a young fellow named Fessenden, pursuing the same elegant occupation as myself. In the course of conversation he told me of his desire to visit certain new openings on the Wardy-allock stream, about twenty miles distant. Before we parted, we entered into an agreement to start together in quest of a richer mine.

Providing myself with provisions and tools, and having notified Perrin of my intention, and placed Clark and the household under his charge until my return, we set off next morning on foot. After a toilsome march over a very mountainous and difficult road, we found ourselves at the creek, in a small ravine or "canon" among the mountain defiles, not far from the great, unexplored, interior desert, and full sixty-five miles from Ballerat, instead of twenty. About a hundred persons were gathered there, but to our inexpressible chagrin, we found there was no gold worth gathering. A few shepherds, who had remained there through the rainy season, had found a scanty deposit in a ravine, the exaggerated fame of which had drawn many to the spot only to be deceived. Such reports are purposely circulated by the traders, who make a good speculation from the needs of the improvident and humbugged people whom they cheat into their neighborhood. As a general thing, provisions are only provided for the journey, and this being three times as long as is expected, they are compelled to repair to the shops to obtain necessities, on their arrival.

Having no particular engagement, Fessenden and myself agreed to take advantage of the trip into the remote and almost unexplored neighborhood, to ramble about in the solitudes of the Australian forests. Among these wild ranges of rough and wooded hills there are no inhabitants, not even "natives," and the kangaroos sport at pleasure. Of these there are different species, some being no larger than a dog; others as large in size as a man.

After some days of this desultory wandering,

we bethought ourselves of the land we had left, and sought to regain it in the same manner we had come — *on foot*. We had seen the country, but made no money, and contracted severe colds, which made us well nigh sick; having had no covering except the rude boughs which constituted our wigwam, and through which the rain poured more copiously than we could have wished. We started at early morn, and followed a route of our own selection, which we judged would bring us over the skirts of Mount Mercy into a direct path.

The sun was not visible; we had no compass; and the result of our experiment was, that after crossing an infinite variety of hills, ravines, swamps, thickets, and woods, we met two men, whom we recognized as friends in the place from whence we had escaped. We inquired, with surprise, how they came to be traveling from the direction of Ballerat, and in reply found, to our greater astonishment, that it was ourselves in that course, being only two miles from Wardy-allock diggings, with a prospect of reaching them. We had been turned about in the woods, and made almost a complete circle. Desirous of avoiding the awkward inquiries we knew must await us if we went forward, we at once turned our steps, and late at night encamped on the verge of the Australian desert, under a gum tree. In the distance we discerned the ungainly mass of Mount Elephant, and the stock road to Adelaide, leading across the plain.

On the morning of the fourth day we reached Ballerat, in no wise richer than when we went; but I found, to my pleasurable surprise, that Clark's foot had entirely healed in my absence, and that he was able to walk nearly as well as ever. Perrin had paid expenses by collecting grains of gold, and by adventures in his profession of peddling, and besides had done considerable business as a sort of commission agent, by procuring for his customers any commodity they might desire. His stock consisted usually of silk dresses and ladies' shoes — articles that, it would seem, would find rather a dull market in a community of miners; but there were thousands of women, a large proportion of whom were profuse in expenditures for dress. Our party of three being now reunited, it again became a matter of serious consultation as to the best method of pushing our fortunes. Thus far we had done but little more than to gain our bare subsistence. While wandering rather disconsolately about Ballerat Flat, considering the question, I saw, at a little distance before me, a tall figure, which I thought I recognized as a fellow-townsman; and, upon approaching nearer, discovered, to my delight, that the well-proportioned figure and fine features were none other than those of Captain W., who had come out to Australia with a heavy invoice of Colt's revolvers. He had tried in vain to effect sales in Melbourne, and had come to the mines hoping to find private sales, but was disappointed at every point, the market being forestalled by clumsy English arms.

I forgot for a time my distress, in the pleasure of hearing of matters and things at home; but once again alone, necessity pressed itself upon me; and we determined to put up a canvas house, obtain a stock of goods, and try the mercantile business. As we were about negotiating for the same, down came the "fifty-pound license law" upon us, effectually dampening our ardor in this direction, for we had scarcely this sum among us all. At this juncture, I suddenly recollected there was not in the whole city of Ballerat, to my knowledge, a single undertaker or coffin maker, while deaths were of daily occurrence. The thing was decided at once. Undertakers would have no license.to pay; and we immediately sent for lumber from Melbourne; threw out a sepulchral-looking white flag to the breeze, upon which was displayed a black coffin, forming a striking contrast to the gay streamers all about it. The day after this we had an order from the friends of a New England man, but could only meet it by buying some old shelves of a dry goods store at half a dollar the running foot. Not long after, the lumber came from Melbourne, at twenty-five cents a foot, and twenty-five dollars cartage for a dray load. We have averaged one coffin a day at prices from eight pounds to seventeen, which latter were finished in English style.

Deaths in Ballerat are almost all from accident or dysentery. Fevers are almost unknown in the pure and bracing air of Australia. The former disease is doubtless induced by the bad water which all are obliged to use. The majority are in the habit of supplying themselves from the yellow, muddy creek, or the blue water of the old shafts. The more particular bring what they use from the singular "lagoons," as they are called, that are frequently found in the vicinity on the tops of high hills, about a mile from our abode.

How refreshing would be a draught of our good old New England streams, that come trickling down the mountain sides, mirroring the trees and flowers on their banks in their transparent bosoms!

The duties of housekeeping, which devolve mainly upon me, together with those of my business, keep my time occupied through the day. I think I shall be prepared to appreciate, very sensibly, the labors of faithful housewives, though the well-appointed machinery, the full storeroom and larders which they deem so necessary to their comfort and convenience, make it vastly easier than the rude implements of our wigwam, and scanty materials for cooking.

CHAPTER X.

ADVENTURES IN BALLERAT. — VISIT CRESWICK CREEK. — POWER OF KINDNESS OVER CONVICTS. — WALKING LEAVES. — LEAVE BALLERAT FOR CALLAO. — HISTORY OF AUSTRALIA.

THE great desideratum of all travelers who are wealthy enough to pay large prices every where, both by land and sea, is fresh provisions. We had not the "available substance," and besides, we had seen the time when money could not have procured for us the "nutritious elements" as we desired, had we been able to offer it ever so lavishly. In default of these things, we found vinegar, or any thing made with it, was eaten with a relish almost like that induced by famine, and was invaluable as opposing the evil effects of long-continued salt diet. Having gathered some experience on this point, one of my first undertakings, upon establishing myself at Ballerat, was to set up a vinegar yard — not a large piece of ground, with long rows of casks, but merely and singly an old bottle, into which I put tea leaves and coffee grounds, filled it with sweetened water, and hung it upon one of the trees about our home, where it might be exposed to the sun. In three or four days I had a bottle of clear and sharp vinegar, which was used with the greatest appreciation, not only at our own table, but at those of others, whom I occasionally favored with a sour gift. Another successful enterprise was the making of hop beer. Perrin, in some of his wanderings or commission errands, discovered a small quantity of hops, sent up on commission, and for which there seemed no possible use. These I eagerly procured — boiled them, "using my judgment," as women say, in the quantity of water, &c., but was utterly at a loss for appropriate flavor. As an experiment, I threw in a quantity of ginger and cayenne pepper; dissolved separately two ounces of soda, and one of cream tartar, stirring in first the alkali and then the acid; and strange as it may seem, in a day or two it became a perfect nectar, for excellence. The pepper, about which I had many misgivings, was the perfect "arcanum" of its glory. We drank moderately ourselves, and now and then presented a bottle to some lady, or particular friend, with a feeling of generosity such as Prince Metternich might experience in sending a dozen of real Johannisbergs to an intimate autocrat. In truth, it was even more choice, for the water at Ballerat could scarcely be drank at all, without being boiled into tea or coffee, and even then it was poor enough.

The keen, Yankee inquisitiveness of Perrin was often of great service to me. "*Grand news* I have brought to you," said he, one day, which turned out to be, that a quarter cask of Indian meal was to be found at a certain grocery. All my New England remembrances came upon me, from the dear delights of hearthstone and friends, down to Johnny cake and Indian pudding. Chiefly stimulated by animal considerations, however, I repaired at once to the spot, saw the treasure as it had been described, inquired about it, carelessly and in an indifferent manner, bought it for a mere song, and bore it home in triumph.

It had come thither no one knew exactly how, had stood no one knew how long, having escaped the eyes of the Yankees, and no one else knew how to use it. It was, indeed, somewhat mingled with moth webs, but it was, nevertheless, a magnificent discovery to us, and a most welcome change.

Provisions of every description are at "gold prices" at Ballerat — flour, sixty dollars a barrel; pies, one dollar each; eggs, half a dollar singly, and other things in proportion; vegetables are particularly scarce and costly.

Longing one day for something that came from the earth, I went in search of some greens. I succeeded to my great satisfaction, bringing home a good bag of common dock; which I boiled, salted, buttered, vinegared, and peppered, — producing a dish, as we thought, worthy a king. Clark, however, like an obstinate fellow, insisted that the "royal mess" might be poisonous, and therefore refused to taste it; but knowing that his scruples would only be our gain, we exhorted him but little. I at once communicated the knowledge to my neighbors; from which time, the dock-digging business was so strenuously prosecuted as entirely to extirpate the weed for a considerable distance round.

29th. Christmas day was observed as one of general jubilee, especially by the English, whom I have every where observed to enjoy their national holidays to the utmost, wherever they may be, especially if the rough side of life be their daily lot. For two whole days work was superseded, and low and uproarious proceedings, by way of rejoicing, were seen in every part of the city. There is no lack of places of amusement, many of the largest tents being exclusively ball and concert rooms. My own part of the "celebration" consisted of a pleasant interview with Mrs. Haynes, a particular friend, and a dinner of the combined nationalities of baked beans and plum pudding. I attended divine service, and while rambling through the streets afterward, I was hailed from one of the tents with "Well, mate!" in a sharp, decided voice.

On looking around me, I discovered that I had been addressed by an Australian magpie, a black and white bird very nearly resembling a bobolink, and having a capacity for distinct articulation far surpassing the parrot. "Well mate," cried the saucy bird again, as I turned and approached its cage, adding, with profane emphasis, " O, you d——d fool!" I left, but he shouted after me in triumph, with the same profane expressions, till I was quite out of hearing. A fearful hurricane of hot wind has swept over us, so strong and stifling as entirely to prevent work in the open air for a time. I was sitting at my tent door when the heavy black clouds arose. They swept down from the mountains, coming near the earth, seemingly encircled with a wreath of fire, that looked more like a conflagration than electricity; so hot and loaded with sand, we were forced to cover our faces in our bed clothes till the strength of the blast was spent. All day long this state of things continued, though with intervals of calm, making breathing almost misery. A few days of such burning sirocco would destroy the whole city. As it is, many of the frail edifices of the miners are among the things that *were*, but *are* not. Nearly fifty tents were torn up and blown away during the day; some of them so suddenly that the surprised inmates were left seated at their tables in the open air.

Our own was only preserved stationary by means of ropes thrown over and attached to piles of lumber on either side. The storm has swept wide, leaving a broad path of desolate blackness behind it. No one is able to speak satisfactorily of the origin and nature of these destructive tornadoes. Some affirm that it comes, bearing heat and fire from some burning forest at a distance.

Others say the qualities are electrical only, and that the storm was generated somewhere within the unknown depths of the great interior desert; but the mysterious and wisely-regulated laws of the great forces of nature are poorly understood by us in our ignorance.

Man may create ingenious theories, speculate and wonder, and only come at last to see that it is pitiable folly.

January 6th, 1854. — Times growing rather dull, and Clark and myself being weary of such a monotonous life in one place, we started for

Creswick Creek, about fourteen miles distant from Yankee Hill. The walk was exceedingly pleasant over gently-undulating ground, and through forests, most of which are comparatively open and pleasant. All the Australian trees are evergreen; a large proportion, however, undergoing a sort of equivalent annual change in shedding their bark. Nearly all the leaves are lanceolated with slight variations, and although, in general, they are set very thickly upon the tree, they yet offer little shade, as they stand edgewise, and therefore oppose only the thickness of the leaf to the rays of the sun.

A singular and frequent shrub in swamps and low grounds is the grass tree, which consists of a radiating bunch of leaves like a coarse grass, from the midst of which rises a straight, woody stem, five or six feet in height, surmounted with a hard, close head, resembling the New England "cat-tail."

We arrived at Creswick about sunset, and camped in sight of the diggings. At a small trading stand where I went to purchase some provisions, I met an old man, who, with some of his boon companions, was sipping the intoxicating cup. I fell into conversation with him, and found him to be a "lag," or convict transported from England. Although somewhat elevated with drink, he yet conversed shrewdly, and I soon became interested in him and his fortunes. He offered me a home in his tent, and freedom to draw from his well-filled purse, as I might need. This confidence, touching and unlimited, was gained simply by the power of kindness, by treating him as a friend, instead of showing contempt for the convict. I doubt not there are many, among the numerous convict population, who, by kind and humane treatment, might be reformed, and become useful citizens.

They possess many good qualities, are open-hearted, boundlessly generous among themselves and those whom they recognize as friends, but hopeless, reckless, and dangerous while treated continually as criminals and outcasts. Returning to my tent one evening, I found, under one of the trees near, a woman apparently about forty years of age, smoking. I gave her a civil salutation, conversed with her a few moments, and went my way. About midnight she came to the tent, put her head inside, and asked, "Is the laddie here who spoke so kindly to me to-night?" "Yes," I replied. "Well! bless his kind heart," said she, "I have come here to thank him for the kind words he spoke. They were the first I have heard for many a long year. I came in the night for fear the police would take me. I'm a poor creature. Once I was a happy woman; but I did wrong, and they sent me away with the worst of rogues, and now I am as bad as any of them. God bless you, my sweet laddie, and keep you from leading such a miserable life." I scarcely knew what reply to make to this outpouring of thankfulness from the unhappy being, but offered a few words more to cheer her troubled spirit. At two o'clock the next night she came again, with a bottle of brandy as a present to her "laddie." I conversed with her for a short time, when she departed for fear of recognition by the police, and I never saw her more. Scarcely any thing is more powerful among men than kindness and sympathy. They subdue a heart into gentleness when sterner means would only harden into insensibility, or, what is worse, give the rein to unbridled passion.

Near the mines at Creswick were encamped a small party of Australian natives — lank, "walnut-headed," almost black, and the most brazen and insatiable beggars imaginable. They were extravagantly fond of our tea, coffee, tobacco, and sugar, and knew English sufficiently to make known their wants. Any thing that was given was instantly secured in their mouths or girdles, and the same importunity manifested the second time, and so on till our patience was exhausted. The natives up the coast, in the neighborhood of Sidney and further, are said to be much more dangerous, revenging upon every white for the wrongs they have suffered from the early emigrants into that region. The race, however, is nearly extinct.

The mines in Creswick are either in very wet, low land, in shafts from ten to thirty feet deep, or in chalk hills of greater depth, where the fine, white dust is intolerable, almost suffocating, and exceedingly unhealthy. The miners come from their work at night, like a regiment of ghosts, perfectly white, and indistinguishable as to features or garments. We spent one day in pecking away at a half-melted conglomeration, where every blow jarred our systems in a manner not altogether agreeable. Thinking such efforts quite too severe for mere speculation, I determined to go back to Ballerat. Clark, who had enough of wilful perseverance to keep him pecking on Mount Washington for gold till the day of his death, was somewhat enraged at this decision, but finally acquiesced, being more inclined to go than to remain alone. Next morning we returned with the reflection uppermost in our minds that a "rolling stone gathers no moss."

It was during this return from the Creek, we saw the celebrated "walking leaves," so called. While sitting under the shade of some gum trees, a slight breeze passed by, which brought to the ground a little shower of leaves. After lying still a moment, they started, and seemed to walk upon their stems toward the trunk of the tree. It is said that some years ago, before Australia was much settled, a party of sailors obtained a few days of liberty to make explorations upon the islands. The first day of their adventure, while sitting in a grove for rest, one of them suddenly cried out, "Let's leave this place at once, or the trees and the land will make off with us. See those leaves marching off on their stems!"

The evidence of their senses seemed sufficient, and there could be no doubt of the inference. They hastened on board the ship, preferring to lose their liberty rather than stay in a region of such doubtful foundation. How full of enigmas is nature to the ignorant and superstitious, making them fear even her happiest and richest manifestations!

16th. — Ballerat is filled with rumors of newly-discovered treasures in Peru, at the head waters of the Amazon, where twenty-five pound "acquisitions" are of every-day occurrence. The Americans are very much excited, and hundreds are daily starting for Melbourne, bound for Callao. They have long been dissatisfied with the extortionate regulations of the English government here. Some of the English sympathize with this restive feeling, though in general they are unanimously arrayed against every thing and every body they call "Yankee;" and this title is given to every one that comes from any part of North America.

We have had a mass meeting of the "lovers of freedom and just legislation," at which were enthusiastic speeches,—some for immediate action, not very plainly indicated,—resulting mainly in the adoption of several fiery resolutions concerning "*fair representation*," &c.; and breaking up with the prevailing sentiment, that "Britons never, never will be slaves." One object, evidently, of the meeting was to retain, if possible, the great numbers that are leaving; but the cry has gone forth, "On for Callao!" and hundreds are rushing, and will still continue to rush, to the new land of golden fame.

We are not uninfluenced by the pervading spirit; beside a coffin-bearing flag, on a tall pole, in a distant part of the city, the escutcheon of an opposition establishment, started during our last absence, relieves us of all apprehensions that our departure would be inconvenient to the community.

Distant and unknown regions have a peculiar charm; and who would not see as much as possible of this wide world? Yes, we will go. Houses and claims are a drug in the market — worth absolutely nothing; but what we have shall be disposed of to the best advantage, and we will start for Melbourne, though it seems, from our original party, I have not a single companion to accompany me on my wanderings. Clark, for a trifling difference, concludes to remain behind. A letter from Yates and Harman, whom we left at the Isle of France, informs us of their arrival at Bendigo, Australia, where they have established themselves in business, as partners in a cookie stand, clearing a net profit of five dollars a day.

We have, after all, done better than the majority in Ballerat, having paid our expenses, and gained some real estate, — at least, by miner's title, — and have enough to carry us to Callao, with a prospect of a little remainder. Probably not more than ten per cent. of the miners obtain a competency, or more; half the remainder collect sufficient to get away with, while twenty-five per cent. of the whole die there, at home, or on the way thither, of diseases contracted here, not so much by reason of climate as the manner of living, which is usually reckless.

20th. — The step is taken, and we are on board the bark Sacusa, bound for Callao, where I have plenty of leisure to review the past, and consider the history of the island we have left.

We started from Ballerat on a route different from that which carried us there; proceeding directly across the country instead of going by Geelong.

At one of our halting places, on the banks of a river, a fine bridge was being built, and near by the grading for a railroad was commenced. From this place to Melbourne was a handsome stone road, built chiefly by convict labor, and constructed after the thorough English fashion; being a layer of rocks of considerable size, carefully laid, firm and close, a second above it of smaller size, and so on until the road is several feet thick, and finally completed with a thick stratum of hard gravel. Among the crowds of workmen who were engaged in continuing or repairing it, were many respectable, intelligent-looking men, perhaps voluntary workmen. Every one at work on the road claims two dollars fifty cents per day and rations, from government; and numbers of unsuccessful miners have resorted to this method as a *surer* way of obtaining gold, though it be not very rapid.

In one instance, we passed through a settlement of English emigrants, who live by farming and providing for the wants of miners, who pass through the district on their way. There was neither church, school house, nor store; and a general appearance of indifference and sloth about the whole place—arising, doubtless, from the fact, that none owned their land, it being held in large grants by noble or wealthy persons, who will not sell, and who lease only on terms which render the tenant little better than a serf. A similar state of things is obstructing the growth of almost all the Australian cities.

Building lots in Melbourne are often held at from fifty to one hundred thousand . dollars each, and rented at ten thousand a year. Land for a garden, three miles out of the city, has sold recently for eighty thousand dollars an acre. Prices in Adelaide are generally high.

Even at Ballerat building lots were sold at auction, some distance from the mines, for fifteen hundred dollars each. The idea of an emigrant settling upon land within a hundred miles of any city, is out of the question. All good land within that distance, if not beyond it, is granted out in "runs," or large grazing farms, which cover a space five to twenty miles in length, including not only all the running water, but all the "lagoons," ponds, and springs, of any value. Without unfailing sources of water, land in Australia would be valueless.

This land monopoly is the source of much trouble; for many intelligent men who have entered the country, with their families, have found the only alternative to be, to hire out to keep stock under these wealthy holders, who, of course, take advantage of the necessity to enhance their own benefit.

The wide streets of Melbourne were a most welcome sight to us, after our confinement to wild forests and muddy or dusty hills or plains. We spent the time allowed us in visiting places of interest, one of the most noticeable of which was the "Emigrant's Home." This was established, with the aid of government, by a few benevolent men, for the relief and assistance of the poor and suffering among this class. There are several large buildings, divided into tenements for different families, with a physician and dispensary attached. Here the sick and the indigent may find a home until recovered from disease, or find employment. A similar, but smaller, institution is sustained by the Wesleyans, and devoted exclusively to that sect.

We also found great pleasure in the quiet solitudes on the banks of the Yarra Yarra, and in visiting the splendid public gardens, wandering about the walks, admiring the graceful swans in the pools, and the spacious greenhouses, with their brilliant and valuable contents.

Australia, as a whole, may be well styled a "land of anomalies." In the words of another writer, "The whole form, character, and composition of this country are so singular, that a conjecture is hardly hazarded before it is overturned; every thing seems to run counter to the ordinary course of nature in other countries. In other lands, the rocks and reefs that run into the sea determine, in many cases, the direction and continuity, or otherwise, of the mountain systems; but the rocks and reefs of Australia afford no such key to the inquirer — they belong not to geology — they are the work of the coral insect, rising perpendicularly from the depths of the ocean till they form ridges and islands above its surface, which have nothing in common with any thing but themselves."

The most remarkable feature in the Australian coast is, the total absence of outlets for any large rivers, thus making the freshness and fertility which usually attend the course of these "great fertilizers," almost unknown. Productive soil is found mostly on the sides and summits of considerable elevations, and those engaged in exploring tours to the interior look for these indications of mountain land, with a longing anxiety, which it is difficult for those to understand who dwell in more favored lands. Another fact, that cannot fail of being observed, is, that these spots, confined to the higher regions, are as effectually separated from each other by apparently irredeemable deserts, as though the ocean flowed between them.

It appears probable, however, that both the land and water are still in a course of formation; that the various anomalies, in each, which fill the minds of so many with wonder and amazement, are only the natural appearances of an imperfect, or rather of an unfinished work, and that they will vanish when the causes now in operation shall have produced their full effect.

Writers profess to hazard these conjectures with much caution, and only because they appear to result from the facts collected by actual observers.

Botany Bay, at its south-eastern point, has received its name, it is well known, from the abundant vegetation which the early discoverers found along its coast. It is scarcely less well known, that the first attempt at colonization was made at this bay, and almost immediately abandoned, under the conviction that its soil was unprofitable and sterile. Such conflicting statements, by able men, seem strange at first sight; but investigation shows them to grow naturally out of the character of the Australian botany, which is as peculiar as most other things in this region of peculiarities. "Picturesque and pleasing," said the considerate pioneer, but "something more than *beauty* must be sought in a place where the permanent residence of multitudes is to be established."

The physical character of the Australian himself is not more marked by a general inferiority than are his moral and intellectual attainments. He ranges through the fields, like man in his primitive state, unclothed; possessing not the smallest knowledge of agriculture, even in its rudest form; has scarcely an idea of arts or manufacture; indeed he may rather be considered as a gregarious than a social animal; for, although some personal respect is sometimes paid to a kind of chief among a tribe, it would seem that it is altogether personal, and independent of any right, either hereditary or elective.

The stupidity of their nature and the inertness of their faculties are evinced by their thoughtlessness and neglect in obtaining food, or to obviate those incessantly recurring attacks of famine to which he has always been exposed.

Though it be going too far, probably, to say that the native is incapable of improvement, the fair presumption seems to be, that he is destined to remain forever in the lowest scale of civilization, and to be inferior in point of comfort, as he has hardly been superior in contrivance hitherto, to many of the lower animals.

Although the Island of Australia, naturally and artificially, presents many jagged and rough points, yet, like every part of God's dominions, it has its features of beauty and interest, and its part to serve in the world's history.

CHAPTER XI.

MONOTONY OF SEA LIFE.—CHANGE IN TIME BY THE OMISSION OF ONE DAY.—LANDING AT SOUTH AMERICA.— DISAPPOINTED HOPES.— STAY AT LIMA.— ROMAN FESTIVAL.

22d. — Yesterday we sighted Van Diemen's Land. We are making south, for the purpose of rounding the southern point of New Zealand and gain some advantage of wind.

Our passengers number about a hundred, and as a whole, are a most agreeable class of men with whom to travel. They are chiefly Americans, English, and Scotch — experienced travelers, many of them having already been to California in search of gold, and still pursuing the phantom of wealth untiringly, although the frosts of many winters have settled upon them, reminding others, if not themselves, that the time draws near when earthly treasures will avail them nothing.

Life on shipboard has in it much of sensuality. Eating becomes a matter of primary and absorbing importance. Monotony and lack of occupation conspire with sharp sea appetites to make the daily meals absolutely the chief points of interest during the day, and these present arrangements bid fair to furnish something more worthy of rational thought than the miserable food and still more miserable conduct on the Peytona, which was indeed a disgrace to humanity.

February 10th. — Since my last record, we have had a comfortless and even dangerous time, by reason of a long-continued gale, which tossed our small vessel more fearfully than we could wish. So violent was the ship's motion, it was impossible to leave our bunks; beside, sundry trunks were loosened from their hold, and were sliding about the cabin in wild confusion. An immense retinue of small articles almost immediately followed — things which their owners had unsuspectingly secreted under their bunks, or laid unfastened upon shelves above. Plates, demijohns, jugs, knives and forks, boots and shoes, cups and bottles — miscellaneous messes of beans, rice, &c., saved for lunch — rolled and danced over the floor in the most indescribable manner, for the space of twenty-four hours, while the gale was at its hight.

For myself, I feel a positive pleasure in traveling with decent people, upon a respectably managed ship. We are not overcrowded; things in the main are satisfactory, and all things go on harmoniously from day to day, without those soul-discomforting events that have hitherto tried us.

We have, however, a set of gamblers on board; seemingly professional gentlemen in that line, who play with scarcely an intermission, except for their meals; keeping it up not only during the day, but through the night also.

Happily, the captain will not allow it on the Sabbath, neither any other amusement; and we have the grateful intermission of at least one day.

Since the return of fair weather our ship's reckoning has been altered, according to the custom of mariners, by omitting one day.

By passing around the world eastward, we should, of course, for each thousand miles of the whole twenty-four of the earth's circumference, come one hour sooner to sunrise, and at our return home by the same route, one day having as it were slipped backward upon the stationary time at home, would have passed over twenty-four full hours, and would be coinciding again with home time, but with this difference: we should be calling it by the name which our friends had used for the day before. Leaving, then, for example, on Sunday, we might reach home on that day, which to us would be Saturday, obliging us to omit one day in our date. This omission is made for general convenience at the meridian of one hundred and eighty degrees longitude, opposite the initial meridian of Greenwich, and therefore the most proper point.

The mysterious extinction of a day caused no little merriment and much speculation. The captain, being able to drop any day he chose, concluded to extinguish the seventh; whether from professional or individual enmity to religion, or to gratify his avaricious disposition by keeping the crew at work, is unknown.

The change was made upon the log-book without any public intimation of it; and we, who were strenuously observing it, by extra ablutions, careful dress, and abstaining from amusements, were suddenly taken aback by seeing things proceed in the usual manner.

The murmuring at this movement of the captain's was so general and so loud, he was glad to ordain the observance of the next day, Tuesday of the new style, as a substituted Sabbath, at least so far as regarded rest from labor, and some other trifling, though to us indispensable ceremonies, according to our own views.

12th. — Our second mate is thoroughly ignorant of every thing except working ship, and, like many others who are profound in a narrow circle of knowledge, and supreme in a small sphere of power, is abundantly vain of his acquirements, and ostentatious of his authority. He is six feet in hight, broad and muscular, with a full, red face, bushy hair, large, dark eyes, with no meaning whatever, and a voice that rings through the ship in a manner that almost makes her tremble. Having exhausted the difficulty naturally attendant upon the commencement of a voyage with a crew out of practice by a year or two of mining, he seems to have concentrated his dislike upon our cabin boy, who has, at best, a temper fiery in the extreme. "Boy Bill," as he is called, is invariably aroused at half past three o'clock, and in such a boisterous manner as to dissipate the slumbers of the passengers for the rest of the night.

The nuisance grew so unbearable, a scheme was formed to prevent it if possible. The morning following its formation, as the mate appeared at the door of the saloon, a forward passenger shouted "Boy Bill," and immediately the same was reiterated to the farther end of the cabin, by seventy-five different voices, with as much power as they could command. The uproar was terrible and deafening, but highly effective, as it has given to us the peaceable hours of rest, undisturbed by the stentorian tones of this "son of thunder."

20th. — We have been forty days out, the average voyage being much less, and have not yet seen any thing of the coast of South America. Some begin to be afraid that our reckoning is wrong; but the captain refuses information, taking it as an insult that any one disbelieves his daily bulletin of latitude and longitude. For the last two or three days there has been much dissatisfaction, which found definite utterance this morning in an anonymous despatch upon the bulletin board, in the form of an advertisement on this wise: —

"LOST, STRAYED, OR STOLEN.

"*The American ship Sacusa, Captain Scott, which left Port Philip for Callao, with one hundred passengers, January 20th. When last heard from, she was near the antipodes; supposed now to be somewhere in the Pacific Ocean, between Australia and America. A very handsome reward will be paid to any who will correctly state her whereabouts, and a still greater one to those who will pilot her into the port of Callao.*

"*In behalf of one hundred sickened passengers.*"

It has excited the ire of the commander, but being impossible to find the instigator of such a movement, nothing will be done.

During the whole of our long voyage, we have not spoken one vessel, nor sighted land since the antipodes — a somewhat uncommon instance of a solitary passage. It has somehow come to the knowledge of the captain that Perrin and myself were passengers in the Peytona, famous through this part of the world as an unlucky ship.

To-day he sent us a polite invitation to visit him; and, thinking such attention not to be declined, we went; gave him an account of our wanderings, much to his surprise and gratification.

"Well!" said he, good-naturedly, at the close of the tale, "I've had a pretty long voyage this time, and no wonder, since I've got two Peytona Jonahs on board. I don't expect to make any port at all now."

March 29th. — Full two days before the coast of South America was visible, those very discerning ones, of whom there are usually a goodly number on board ship, could see distinctly "the loom of the land," and even the very peaks of the long-looked-for Andes. These airy visions kept up considerable excitement, both among the credulous and those who made sport of it. Whenever any one has been specially confident of seeing the shadow in the eastern horizon, or the faint outlines of some snowy peak, some one has stood ready to corroborate his statement, and even give it a more tangible form. "Certainly! I see 'em," has been the reply. "Don't you see that mountain covered with trees, and the birds and monkeys in their branches?" and, "Can you not perceive that rock at the foot of the mountain, and a frog upon the top of it?"

Thus the jokers joked; the anxious gazed so sick with suspense they could neither eat nor sleep, while the cooler and more philosophic quietly waited for a solid foundation to their hopes. At last the land was clearly to be seen before us, this morning, in a line of snow-covered peaks, distant and dim, like a dream, and the darker range of highlands below, stretching out of sight on either hand.

Every body was on deck,—officers, crew, and passengers,—for the morning was perfect and the sight lovely. About noon, to the confusion of all the unbelieving despisers of the captain's skill as a navigator, the roadstead of Callao came in sight directly before us, into which he brought the ship as accurately and fairly, as if he had drawn her thither by a line; but the critics, like all mistaken ones, insisted upon it that the success was pure accident, and no credit to the captain.

It was a strange and eager crowd that covered the deck as we ranged slowly up toward the anchorage. There stood the gamblers, some of them penniless, and others correspondingly rich with their gains. By their side were men with gray hairs and wrinkled faces, who had been first to California, afterward to Australia, in unsuccessful search after gold, leaving families in narrow circumstances at home — their lives thus far a failure, and their one remaining hope, that of making up for all in the new diggings of Peru. No small number had laid out every dollar they possessed in the world for this passage, and a meager outfit for the journey to the mines on the Amazon.

There, too, was Williams, a young man who had been brought on board apparently far gone with the consumption, but who has recovered a considerable share of health and strength in the balmy air of the Pacific; looking forward with a dim and half-painful hope of being at last able to realize the fondest wish of his heart—that of affording material assistance to his father. He was the son of a wealthy Englishman, and was educated with the design of succeeding his father in business; but the latter, becoming bankrupt, removed to a distant country, and he was obliged to abandon school and engage in some effort that would afford some remuneration. His health failed, and to reëstablish it he made the voyage to Australia. Proving favorable, he commenced business there, but was again arrested by symptoms of pulmonary disease, which compelled him to leave, and incidentally brought him on board our ship, still retaining the absorbing desire to aid his father; exhibiting an admirable spirit of filial devotion, seldom witnessed.

The position which I occupied upon the forecastle gave me an opportunity of studying the countenances of the passengers, most of which betokened a vague, uneasy excitement, sometimes of painful intensity. Not a word was said, except in an occasional low whisper, for every man was absorbed with his own individual hopes and fears; but the impatience of the silent throng was manifested more clearly than words could have shown it, by the steady, bent brows, the restless movements, and quiet sighs that unconsciously escaped from nearly all.

The custom-house officer came on board, and the established etiquette barely restrained us from infringing upon his business interview with the captain. This over, the storm of questions was instant and tremendous. "Gentlemen," replied the official, "there is nothing in it; you have all been humbugged." At this brief and unexpected answer a change came over the faces of the crowd, almost like blotting the sun from the heavens in appearance. I saw tears in the eyes of strong men, and an agony of bitter and hopeless disappointment in many more. Some silently went below to weep; some flew into a rage, and swore revenge upon the man who had originated such reports; a few looked merely sullen, and still fewer indifferent.

As for myself and Perrin, we had talked over the prospect many times, and had come to the conclusion that the probabilities of obtaining gold were against us; and our hopes, in consequence, had not become very strong. Beside, it was not so much the hope of gain that had brought us thither, as the love of wandering; which, I confess, was so powerful a principle with me, as to make me comparatively indifferent to poverty or riches.

Upon further inquiry it was ascertained, that the original report was, undoubtedly, founded on assertions of Lieutenant Herndon, of gold to be found upon the head waters of the Amazon, and elsewhere, east of the Andes. The fellow who had spread the news in Melbourne was probably associated with some unprincipled captains or owners, who were desirous of contriving paying voyages for their vessels, then lying unemployed in Port Philip harbor; and letters which he presented, purporting to be from a brother in Peru, containing glowing accounts of the mines, were a base fabrication. We are told that this same man, while coming across upon another vessel, has been caught in robbing a passenger, and is now imprisoned in Callao, to answer to the charge — an item of information that seems a real consolation to many of our unfortunate men, especially considering the misery of Spanish prisons, and the dilatoriness of their tribunals.

The whole number of men thus caught in this net is over two thousand. Callao is full to overflowing of those who are waiting for a steamer to take them to Panama, or staying because they have no money wherewith to take them to a new destination. And worse than all, as I learn from an acquaintance that has come on board, the yellow fever is among them, and hundreds are dying.

Gold, he says, may probably be found in some places near the upper waters of the Amazon, several hundred miles distant; but the journey is, perhaps, as perilous as could be made in South America. It lies across the Andes, through large tracts of the low-land forests; through territories of hostile tribes,

DISCOURAGING PROSPECTS.   237

whose secret assaults and poisoned weapons are sure destruction for small parties. It is certain the trip can not be made at all, except by strong companies, every man completely equipped with arms and provisions for a long expedition — requisites out of the reach of the vast majority of those here.

30th. — After the disheartening news of yesterday, we thought best to remain on board for the night; and this morning we went on shore, to see who of our Australian acquaintances might be found. Three of the passengers have joined Perrin and myself, and despite our cloudy prospects we are quite cheerful, and determined to keep together and make the best of it. We were met at every turn by scores of those who had arrived before us, and on the principle that "misery loves company," were delighted to see us. Doleful were the details that we heard from each and all; living was expensive, board exorbitant, houses were full; no one dared venture for the mines; no ships were up for California, or the Isthmus; no steamer would leave for Panama for two or three weeks.

This was truly a melancholy story for us; but considering despondency a sure road to the fever, and not being quite penniless, we resolved to look about Callao, and inquire for lodgings. In wandering about the different hotels, I found a letter from Mrs. Haynes, one of our party from Geelong to Ballerat, who had preceded me, and was already on her way to San Francisco. She advises me to go at once to Lima, and remain until an opportunity is offered to sail for Panama, and I am inclined to do so.

Callao is low, flat, and sickly; the streets narrow and intolerably filthy; the houses mean and poor, with mud walls and flat roofs. One of the first and most remarkable things that attracted our attention, was the immense pile of wheat that was to be seen in the open air. Thousands of bushels are piled together in this situation, remaining an almost incredible time without injury, there being no rain on this coast, and consequently a dry atmosphere.

The present town is of comparatively modern origin; the former having been wholly submerged and destroyed in a terrible earthquake in 1746, which also laid waste a part of Lima.

It is said that many portions of buildings still standing can yet be seen at low water. Immense treasures were buried in private dwellings, and more in the large churches which still lie among the ruins "in the bottom of the sea." Various applications have been made for permission to seek for them, but for some unknown reason the Peruvian government has invariably refused.

April 13th. — The excitement consequent upon life in Lima has left me neither time nor inclination for daily journalizing. Two weeks have been spent in rambling about the city; and from this *stand-point* I can speak of that which my eyes have seen and my ears have heard, with more satisfaction to myself, and perhaps greater benefit to others.

With several of our ship's company we came to Lima, a distance of ten miles, being an ascending grade of fifty feet to the mile, in about one hour.

The cars here are mere open carriages — no

protection from the rain or cold being necessary. The sun sent down upon us his scorching rays; but the road is in immediate proximity to the old government road, which is shaded on either side with magnificent trees, whose broad branches afford an agreeable shade.

Upon our arrival, we found that our expenses would not vary much from six dollars a week — a sum altogether too large for our limited resources, especially as we had a long journey yet before us. After a night of rest, we sallied forth, satisfied our wants with bananas from the market place, and finally succeeded in obtaining cheap lodging rooms of a German landlord, where we established ourselves, and very soon felt at home. We thought of encamping somewhere in the neighborhood, but found the country entirely inclosed; beside, the vicinity swarms with robbers, and straggling soldiers, identical with them, who rob and murder at their pleasure. A large number of American and English people are here, and their affinity of blood and language seems to bring them together as breth-

ren of one family, laying aside the distinction that existed in Australia, or forgetting differences by being in a common condition of poverty in a strange land.

Lima looks somewhat imposing as approached from the ocean; standing out prominently upon an elevated table-land, and this upon the dark background of the Andes. The mountains in this region are quite barren — all the upper portion of the first range, a mile or two from the city, being a mere mass of lava, while the land at their base is a garden of tropical vegetation. Scores of churches, convents, and cathedrals tower above the lower buildings, and give a powerful impression of massive grandeur at the first view. Ordinarily, the houses are but one story, with flat roofs, so constructed by reason of frequent earthquakes, which render them liable to be thrown down; and they are incomparably less dangerous under these circumstances, than if they were more elevated and of solid material. Sun-dried bricks, made of clay and chopped straw, form the bulk of their building stuff. Lima contains about seventy churches, besides the grand cathedral which stands in the plaza, and was built by Pizarro, being one hundred and eighty-six feet in front by three hundred and twenty deep. It is considered a fine specimen of architecture, but much dilapidated; and indeed, in its best estate, was sadly injured by gaudy coloring and grotesque ornaments — a plain indication of the want of civilization and refinement in the vain architects. It possesses, at present, no other attractions but a quantity of relics, and some old paintings and statuary. In 1746 its towers were thrown down by an earthquake, but were rebuilt in 1800. It has several fine toned bells, and the wealth which has at different times been lavished upon its interior is scarcely to be credited, except in a city which once paved a street with ingots of silver to do honor to a new viceroy. As a proof of the abundance of silver ornaments, it is said that in 1821, a tun and a half of silver was taken from the various churches in Lima, without being missed, to meet the exigencies of the state.

The Church of San Francisco contains an altar, also built by Pizarro, purporting to stand upon columns of solid silver, beside being decorated with profuse ornaments of silver and gold, and the whole surmounted with a golden statue of himself. The *forms* of these things are certainly to be seen, but the real substances were stolen during the revolution, leaving nothing but base metal gilded over. This church was once the richest in the world, and still retains enough of ornament, painting, and statuary, to render it interesting. There are two large theatres, only one of which is assisted by government, and this is now closed on account of political troubles.

Beside the festivals and dramatic amusements, a favorite evening pleasure of the people of the city consists in promenading upon the grand plaza, which is a spacious, handsome square, lined with all the principal shops, and therefore quite lively. Its sidewalks are handsomely paved with mosaic, while those opposite the cathedral present the novel and startling appearance of being inlaid here and there with human bones, though no one, as I could find, is able to tell whence they came, or why they were there. About a mile distant from this place, across the River Rimac, there is another public square, usually called the Alameda; situated between a range of fine residences on one side and a low wall along the river on the other side, shaded throughout by the choicest tropical trees, thus forming an exceedingly pleasant resort for the lovers of pleasure.

The climate is pleasant, the extremes of heat and cold being never experienced. The thermometer in the city, and in the shade, never falls in winter under sixty degrees Fahrenheit, nor rises in summer above eighty-two degrees, its usual station being about eighty degrees in well-aired apartments.

There are about seventy-five thousand inhabitants in Lima; Spanish and Peruvian by blood, with a small intermixture from other nations. A larger part of the lower classes are Peruvians, mostly indolent and stupid, caring little or nothing for society; even remaining unmoved at the extravagant stories of the gold fields, or the general rumor of a movement upon the city, by rebels of some kind. Their wants are merely sensual, and a bare living suffices. Fruit, which is excessively cheap; a little corn or manioc-root flour; a fine outside garment, in addition to their usual scanty dress, will satisfy all their worldly desires.

There is in the city a small circle of proud and exclusive families of old Spanish blood, who are very wealthy, owning, as we are told, a great part of the city, and large estates in the country, as well as interests in the silver mines. They are seldom out alone after dark, for fear of assassination, as the common people regard them with only malicious feelings.

Many of them are well educated for this country, in a college established at this place, and chiefly patronized by them. They are very tenacious of their old customs, and strangers find it almost impossible to gain access to their circles.

The best portion of the citizens, and, as I believe, of the Peruvians in general, is the large middle class of tradesmen, mechanics, and small land-holders. These people have some spirit; do something for their country; but are excessively fond of dress and amuse-

21*

ments; yet hospitable, courteous in manner, and especially polite and attentive to strangers. Detachments of troops are almost daily to be met, drilling on the public grounds. They are the tamest looking soldiers imaginable, with not nearly as much uniformity in size or skill as is usually seen in our volunteer school-boy companies; nerveless and stupid beyond description. This excites but little surprise, when we consider that they are poor, lower-class natives, pressed into the service, neither knowing nor caring for whom or what they fight.

There are said to be about three thousand priests in Lima, and nuns not less in number. The churches are generally open for mass in the morning, and we have several times attended the service for the purpose of enjoying the music and the coolness of the large, dim buildings. The priests were exceedingly civil, and appeared to court the presence of strangers, more probably for the sake of their contributions than from any other motive. One of the fathers always stands at the door with a plate, and no one can resist giving him at least "a real," if it is only to witness the extreme politeness of the cunning fellows. They are vehement in the affirmation that all such collections go into the church treasury for repairs, replacing images, &c.; but charity hardly forbids the suspicion that a large proportion of it goes for the support of the clergy themselves. The priests are by no means prepossessing in appearance; have neither respectability nor dignity. They may be seen lounging at church doors, even during *divine service*, chatting, laughing, smoking; and, in spite of all this, continue to exert great influence on the lower classes, which constitute the great body of the community. The wealthy and aristocratic occasionally pay some regard to the forms and ceremonies of exterior religion, for fashion's sake, or to avoid dangerous collisions with the priests and their flocks; but at heart they are chiefly infidels.

On the Saturday previous to Palm Sunday we were accidentally present at a curious rehearsal of the exercises for the festival. We had attended service in the morning, and were examining some paintings and statuary in a distant part of the gallery, when the small congregation quietly dispersed, while we were made aware of being locked in by the shutting of the doors. We would have applied for liberty, but observing that preparations were being made in the body of the church for some ceremony, we at once determined to be silent spectators.

Quietly creeping to a front corner of the gallery, we looked and listened, while the farce below proceeded. It proved to be the preparatory drill of one detachment for the grand procession of the following day.

The music and the chanting were solemn and beautiful, and the whole procession, filing about through the vast, dim aisles, and under the lofty roof, with splendid costumes, glittering silvered palm-branches, censers, and all the paraphernalia of a Catholic festival, might have been profoundly impressive. But the actors, numbering fifty, were of all ages, from gray-haired men down to mere boys, and went through their parts with silly laughter, ridiculous grimaces, and tricks, as if they had been a company of monkeys, instead of professedly Christian people commemorating a solemn incident in the life of Christ, their Master.

They pulled each other slyly by the gown, smote each other about the ears and on the shaven crown with the dry, rattling palm-branches, joked and laughed until every thing sacred and impressive had disappeared in the display of levity, folly, and blasphemy.

The procession on the following day was one exceedingly imposing. It was headed by a detachment of several thousand troops, after whom came the bishop and his long train of splendidly arrayed acolytes and clergy, and concluded by an army of citizens. Full a hundred thousand people must have been here on that day, including troops and country people. The long line was gay with banners, military music and uniforms, crosiers, staves, censers, and the waving and flashing of gilt and silvered palm leaves which both men and images bore in their hands. Towering high above all were the images of Christ and the twelve apostles, in fine ruffled shirts and modern outer garments, and in front the representation of the Virgin Mary, dressed in embroidered satin, fancy crape shawl, ribbons, and diamonds. The whole display was certainly very imposing, and the aspect of the whole city exceedingly lively and gay—a state of things which doubtless serves an important purpose in keeping the people quiet and contented under the yoke, both of their priestly and political rulers.

CHAPTER XII.

THE YELLOW FEVER. — VOYAGE TO PANAMA. — ARRIVE AT SAN FRANCISCO. — SCENES AT THE POST OFFICE. — SITUATION OF THE CITY. — IMPRESSIONS OF DIFFERENT MEN.

IF "variety is the spice of life," as some affirm, then the portion of existence which fell to us in Lima was well seasoned. Days and weeks passed while we were strolling about the city, making little expeditions here and there, taking an occasional trip to Callao by railroad, and enjoying social intercourse with our fellows in misfortune. For myself, I fell in with a Swiss gentleman of much intelligence, who kindly invited me to his house, affording me pleasurable seasons, that will ever remain among the pleasantest reminiscences of my stay in the city. That joy and sorrow, pain and pleasure, are closely allied in this world, is not only a theory, but an actual fact, and so felt, as we reviewed scenes and events while on the steamer, bound for Panama.

May 5th. — The agreeable excitement, consequent upon rambling and sight-seeing in Lima, almost prevented us from taking note of the continued ravages of the yellow fever among the foreigners. At last it began to invade our own circle of acquaintance. More than once, when we had passed a delightful evening with a small party, upon inquiring next day of some member for the health of another, we were met with the reply, "He is buried." Not many such shocks were needed to cast gloomy shadows around us, awaking feelings that may perhaps have tended to prepare us for an attack of the same deadly disease. One after another of our circle were at length taken down, myself the last — induced probably by fatigue and watching with my companions. It may have been sheer insensibility that made me confident I was not near death, though a victim of the dreadful fever; but I am inclined to ascribe the calmness and freedom which I felt to a higher than human power or agency; even to that *grace* which "soothes the troubled mind" under the most adverse circumstances of life. My first greeting to the physician, a clever young German, upon his first visit, was, "Well, doctor, I'm not going to die yet!"—positiveness that provoked a smile, and the remark that, "With that disposition you will do well enough." His treatment in all cases was invariably the same—a moderate dose of calomel, blue pill afterward, and citric acid as a cooling drink whenever needed. I swallowed the first, received each installment of the second with great respect, and threw it under my bed in his absence, and drank the refreshing solution of acid with much pleasure. A few days sufficed to complete the work of recovery; and so pleased was my physician with my apparent good behavior, he only presented a bill of the mere cost of the drugs, and declared more than half of the fatal cases would have recovered if they had done the like. I had remained here nearly a month before the expected steamer came up the coast. In company with my friend Williams, from whom the fever seemed to have driven away all consumptive symptoms, but who had lost rather in the struggle between two such foes, I engaged passage for Panama. Perrin, my faithful friend and constant companion and partner from the Isle of France to Australia, thence to Lima, remained behind in order to negotiate, in some way, for a passage home. One of our party was hopelessly ill of the fever; indeed, could not have been more than an hour or two from his death when we were forced to leave him, to reach the steamer.

In spite of the discouraging accounts of the Peruvian mines, and of the route thither, several parties were organized to reach them. During our stay three bands started, each person with a mule, and all the arms and outfit required. Of these, as I learn, one has disappeared forever, in the frightful mountains and forests, having never been heard from after leaving Lima. The second made considerable distance, losing more than half their number, when they were overtaken by about as many of the third party, being all that were left alive.

The two forlorn detachments joined, and for

fear of hostile Indians avoided all human habitations, living during many days of toilsome journeying only upon monkeys and wild oranges. This unhealthy diet, together with swamp atmosphere, bad water, discouragement, and excessive fatigue, obliged them to halt in the depths of the forest. It was then agreed that those who felt able and desirous of doing so, should push on, and that the rest should recruit and return. Some twenty or more proceeded; twelve turned back, eight only reaching Lima, in a wretched condition, — bareheaded, barefooted, tattered, emaciated, penniless, almost starved, — with barely enough of life left to try to preserve it.

This whole emigration from Australia is one vast failure. Probably, of the four thousand men who have come across, not one fifth ever started for the mines, and nearly one third died of fever. The rest gradually scattered, some to Australia, some to California, and others elsewhere. It may be imagined that the threats against the author of this wide-spread sorrow and misery were deep and frequent. No attempts were made, however, to fulfil them, and the miserable man, no doubt, found a sufficient punishment in the squalid rigor of his imprisonment. He was released before we left, and we saw him more than once sneaking about alone, pale and sickly, and with every appearance of shame and sorrow.

Our steamer is the Santiago, the English mail vessel between Valparaiso and Panama — an iron boat, long, narrow, and so low that, sitting over the edge of the guards, our feet nearly touch the water. The accommodations are excellent, and the table luxurious. Having the curiosity, a day or two since, to count the different articles of food at dinner, I found them to be seventy-two, independent of fruit. These quiet days are exceedingly delightful; this portion of the Pacific is as smooth as any inland lake; even a skiff might make a voyage between Lima and Panama. The air is balmy and spring-like; the steamer glides steadily and quietly; and the easy, pleasurable life soothes our very hearts, wearied and worn with such long-continued toils and wanderings.

I find quite a number of English families on board, apparently making the trip for pleasure; and surely they could not have made a better choice.

If American pleasure-seekers would find the object for which they search, they can most assuredly realize it in this region. A summer excursion from New York to Panama, down the coast to Lima or Valparaiso and back, and then to San Francisco home again, would be indeed a trip full of delightful interest.

Panama, May 30th. — Upon reaching Panama, we went first to a hotel, and having seen poor Williams comfortably settled, went out to search for cheaper lodgings ourselves. While in a bar room, my eye was attracted by a card bearing the name of Rev. Mr. Rowell, the American missionary chaplain stationed here. I at once conceived the idea of consulting with him both in regard to our stay and the means of reaching San Francisco, whither we intended to go. After some search, I discovered his residence — a pleasant home in the suburbs of the city, where we were hospitably received, in Mr. R.'s absence, by his wife. While conversing with her, the missionary himself came in, and upon our stating our errand, we received the unwelcome intelligence that the steamer had just left, and we should be under the necessity of remaining in Panama two or three weeks. He kindly offered to lodge us during our stay, in such style as his narrow means would permit, affording nothing but a cool matted floor, on which to rest; but this was at once luxury and economy, and we accepted the offer very gratefully.

In our wanderings about the city, we discovered a "restaurant" very fortunately; and from this time we have invariably taken our meals there. We have carefully avoided speaking of the place to others, lest we make difficulty for the hostess; for we have not been slow in perceiving that it is a select place, even for the better class of priests — an infallible sign of its professional merits.

We met unfriendly looks and words from these fathers at first, a little significant, seemingly, causing us to note them; for they are doubly inimical to foreigners of heretical belief, and in this country the sentiments of the priests are the sentiments of the people. My friend and myself are far from being rich, and our meals are consequently frugal indeed — a fortunate necessity for us, however, as the diseases of northern men in tropical climates are almost invariably the result of intemperance in eating or drinking, or both. We each pay a dime for breakfast, which consists of a cup of excellent coffee, and a nice French roll; two or three dimes for dinner, which is made up of some light dishes, with an abundance of delicious fruit.

The American dime has quite supplanted the "real" as the chief small-change coin on the Isthmus and in California. As for cents, instead of being objects of contempt and aversion, as in the Southern and Western United States, they are objects of curiosity. I have seen a young man carry one on his watch-chain, as "charms" and trinkets are worn at the East, and it has commanded universal attention. "What's that?" is a frequent question. "Why, that must be a cent!" and it is inspected with as much curiosity as if it had been coined by Tubal-Cain, in the original antediluvian mint.

But to return to the restaurant, which is delicately neat, considering the variety and number of its occupants. They seem to constitute a "happy family," much more remarkable than the incongruous animal assemblage sometimes so called. According to our careful and repeated census, there are ducks, hens, turkeys, cats, dogs, goats, pigs, girls, boys, women, and numberless withered Spaniards, all running in and out, at work, play, or sleep, on the ground floor of the low, large room. Among this strange and heterogeneous crowd, cool, and undismayed by the indescribable mixture of voices of beasts and birds, human conversation, calls of customers, the complex responsibilities of the cooking department, which steamed at the further side of the room, and the current calls of the household, this managing partner of the concern goes to and fro upon her innumerable errands; never hurried nor worried — a very pearl of native women. She is immensely fat, with a clear olive skin, fine features, splendid black eyes, pearly teeth, and no small quantum of good nature and dignity.

STATE OF MORALS.

Old Panama, the ancient Spanish city, is quite ruined, and indeed the new place, by the same name, is scarcely less so. Many of the churches show signs of vast wealth in the past, but only a very few families of wealth are in the place now, and neither enterprise nor thrift exists but what is planted here by means of the transit travel to and from California, and down the coast. Americans who establish themselves in business at this point show their characteristic energy, but the natives are never stimulated to follow their example; but, on the contrary, they dislike them and their ways, and if they dared, the intrusive, restless, and monopolizing foreigners would quickly be expelled from the country.

The people in general, numbering somewhere about ten thousand, are mostly low Spanish half-breeds, who live in old ruined houses and bamboo huts, appearing more ignorant, indolent, and vicious than any of their race I have ever seen. The moral and social atmosphere of the place speaks strongly of "barbarism;" even the marriage relation is hardly respected or formally observed.

Mr. Rowell is making great and praiseworthy efforts at reform in this respect, as well as others, and he has, to some extent, succeeded in introducing the practice of the marriage rite, and of conjugal faithfulness, while there are some indications that public opinion will eventually support him.

The religion of Panama is the lowest phase of Romanism. There are a few of the higher ranks who are infidels, associating not at all with the commonalty or the priests, either in society or religious services. Their absence from church ceremonies may, perhaps, be plausibly excused, on the ground of danger; for the few church edifices that continue to be opened for use are so ruinous that they seem ready to fall, at any moment, upon the heads of the deluded worshipers.

There is reason to hope that this clashing of material interests, and the exhibition of superior activity, will rouse the inactive Spanish population to efforts worthy their noble blood, and of the ancient fame of their grand old nation.

The ghastly specters remaining from Lieutenant Strain's frightful expedition across the Isthmus, have arrived at this place. Such bent and feeble frames, such deadly-looking countenances, I have never associated with living men before. One of the number has died, and was followed to his grave in the cemetery by a large number. This burial place is a dreary, unattractive spot, overrun with briers and almost impenetrable thickets of tropical shrubs and vines. We have spent considerable time in searching out and reading inscriptions upon the monuments which affection has sent from the United States, to mark the last resting place of friends in this remote region. Almost all those who have died here are young men, in the prime of life, seized and cut off on their way to California by the dreaded Isthmus fever.

The native inhabitants, as in Italy, destroy the bodies of their dead with quick-lime, casting the slender relics into a pit, when the work of the caustic is complete. While wandering in a solitary and remote spot, I discovered a small, blackened, and barren area, which seemed to have been used for this purpose. Upon it was a small pile of human remains, like moist cinders and gray ashes, with here and there a fragment of bone — relics of existing barbarism. Notwithstanding so much darkness and ignorance, the hope of gain will still influence many to come hither, losing sight of these forbidding features in the eagerness of accumulating wealth, thus confirming the sentiment of the great poet of nature, "How quickly the human heart falls to revolt when gold becomes its object!"

June 15th. — In San Francisco at last. It was only till the last moment that we were able to negotiate for a passage at a rate within our means. About seventy-five of our fellow Australian voyagers came with us, some of whom had money, which they freely dispensed to their poorer companions. Such traits of noble generosity are more common among the large class of roving travelers that have sprung up since the gold discoveries, than many are apt to imagine. It affords pleasant confirmation for the belief that in the lowest class of men, that is, in the least intelligent and cultivated, there are yet redeeming qualities, that speak a certain native goodness of heart. The voyage to San Francisco (usually known, "for short," in California and on the coast, as "Frisco,") occupied twelve days and a half, void of incident worth noting. The excitement of the passengers, as we passed within the Golden Gate, was intense. Cheer after cheer was given from one party and another, evidently prompted by pure exultation at reaching the land of gold, or at being able to tread American soil once more. Many of our company had left California three years before, to do better in Australia. To such the change in the city must have been startling; for where they had left long lines and groups of sand hills and barren hights, the ground was now leveled and graded, streets laid out and crowded with houses, churches, and stores. So great was the change, so striking the improvement, they professed it to be more like an enchanted dream than a reality. A range of handsome private residences has been shown to me on Rincon Point, on both sides of a level and commodious plank road, and surrounded with beautiful gardens, rich in verdure, whose site had been sand hills within three months; so rapid are the works of man, and the operations of nature in this region of vivid life and tremendous energy!

We sailed slowly through a forest of masts, past a long succession of thronged and busy wharves to the steam-ship landing; and as we approached the spot, the immediate vicinity, and all the adjacent streets, as far as we could see, were one compact mass of men and women, eagerly watching, and impatiently waiting to welcome friends whom they expected. Such a host of anxious countenances are seldom seen; and as soon as we were within hailing distance, handkerchiefs were waving in the air from both ship and shore, and innumerable voices were calling each to some friend whom they recognized in the crowd.

Numbers were overcome at the sight of loved ones, from whom they had been long absent; and when the gang-way was laid down, the rush into arms, the tempest of joy and grief, laughter and tears, was affecting in a high degree, beside being inconvenient almost to danger. The arrival of the Isthmus steamers, with their burden of joyous and heavy hearts, with their "silent messengers," bearing gladness or heaviness to so many more, are great events in California. The scene at the post office, on these occasions, is almost without a parallel in the world. The mail arrangements are not yet perfected throughout the interior, and for this reason, coupled with the fact of their wandering, uncertain life, numbers of miners have their letters sent to the city, and come thither for them when they are due. All the business correspondence also comes through these mails, and the result is such a pressure at the delivery office as can scarcely be conceived. There are several windows arranged by an alphabetical series of initials, and from each of these, by daylight of the morning of "steamer days," the line of expectants begins to form, and grows continually, stretching around for a hundred and fifty rods in every conceivable direction, insomuch that a bird's-eye view of San Francisco post office, on steamer days, would afford no unfair representation of California people and their manners.

Some speculating geniuses take advantage of this tedious process to earn money, as Fabius saved Italy, by the delay. The rule "first come, first served," is rigidly enforced, and they come early to the ground, secure a station near the window, pretty certain of an opportunity to sell their right of succession to some hurried or anxious merchant for five or ten dollars. Often the purchaser can much better afford this payment than to waste a whole day, perhaps more, in hanging round the office, or "standing on a string." A less direct and honorable mode of evading the difficulty is often practiced, which has been the cause of much reasonable complaint and annoyance. In California women are treated with marked distinction and deference, more so than in any other country in the world, without exception. Of course there is a particular window for them at the office, and especially obliging and active clerks; and in order to avail themselves of the advantage, numbers of merchants are in the habit of having their letters directed to their wives, instead of themselves. Thus many a fair agent—sometimes really a wife, and sometimes only a hired substitute for the occasion — enables her lord to read his letters and act accordingly, many hours before his wifeless, less enterprising, or more fair-minded competitors.

What a study is human nature! How every phase of it appears to the traveler — sometimes in a manner that elicits profound admiration, and again exciting scarcely less than disgust! Nothing very strange if Young had similar experience, ere he penned the line, —

"How *abject*, how *august* is man!"

Here to this famed and youthful city I have come, with what design I can scarcely tell, — not to dig in the bowels of the earth for golden treasures merely, nor to engage in any other branch of business in particular, but rather to gratify a love of wandering, — hardly any thing more definite than to see what there is to be seen, and, perchance, become a " doer," provided a congenial situation presents itself.

My money is nearly gone, but I find a welcome home with my brother-in-law, already established in this place, and propose to remain to look about the city, and then take a look at the northern mines of gold, up the valley of the Sacramento, in the skirts of the Sierra Nevada.

20th.—I have been so particularly fortunate as to meet in the city an old friend and fellow-townsman, who has very kindly acted as my guide and conductor to all points of interest in and about the city; but these have been so generally described by travelers, I shall omit extended individual notices, and remark only the general features of the city and its location. From Telegraph Hill, the highest point in San Francisco, we command a view of the whole city and suburbs; the wharves and shipping of the whole bay, its islands and shores. The city occupies the inner slope of the southern of those two points, between which is that magnificent entrance to the bay, called the Golden Gate. To the westward rises the low chain of hills which shut out the view of the Pacific; while close beneath us, to the north-east, east, and south-east, spread the streets and squares of the city, with their gardens crowning the whole with peculiar and rare beauty. The bay shore is lined with docks, and a great crowd of shipping — vessels of all forms and sizes, on whose tall masts hundreds of flags, of all nations are gently waving in the breeze, We can look directly down to Rincon Point, through Montgomery Street, while from others comes a distinct view of the bay. All the grades are easy and even; the streets wide and straight; but it must be confessed the chief and characteristic feature of the whole is the large number of comfortable houses, surrounded with green and pleasant gardens. Among the prominent buildings is the substantial and ornamental custom house; the Romish cathedral, conspicuously erected upon the very best location in the city, and several Presbyterian churches. Numerous others, smaller and of less moment, appear; but the whole view impresses the observer with an idea of life, vigor, and busy enterprise — comparatively in its infancy, to be sure, but not less decided, inspiriting, and hopeful for the future, than New York with its bay and suburbs. Steamers are constantly leaving the docks, laden to their utmost capacity with freight and passengers, for the Sacramento, Stockton, Petaluma, Napa, Sonoma, San Jose, and the Contra-Costa settlements, in the latter of which farms and country houses form an agreeable feature of the landscape. The power of well-directed energy to transform the wild places of the earth into a garden of beauty, — even a terrestrial paradise, — is fully manifest here. The superficial gazer looks upon what human achievement hath wrought, and is lost in amazement; the man of calculation looks abroad, and revolves in his mind some successful scheme by which his own name will be identified with the increasing glory; while the thoughtful, serious observer witnesses the scene, and wonders if the regenerating influence of truth and right will come soon enough, and powerful enough, to save it from the doom of proud, imperial Rome, in other times.

Thus, according to the constitution of different minds, are different emotions awakened in the beholders of every scene.

CHAPTER XIII.

IMPRESSIONS OF LIFE AT SACRAMENTO CITY. — STAY AT CAPTAIN PIKE'S HOME. — MUD AND DIAMOND SPRINGS. — SCHOOL HOUSES. — MAMMOTH TREES. — INFLUENCE OF CURIOSITY.

Sacramento, June 28th. — While rambling about the streets of San Francisco, gathering information of the mines, I fell in with an old shipmate from the Sacusa, Captain Pike, a man even more impatient and roving than myself. Having become tired of city life, he proposed to me to join our forces in an excursion to the northern mines; and consenting to the arrangement, our small preparations were speedily made, and we embarked together on the steamer for Sacramento City. The travel between the city and the mining districts is always large. We had on board several hundred passengers, and a large quantity of freight. On our way across the bay, to the mouth of the river, we passed several desolate-looking islands and high rocks, rendering the appearance of the coast barren in the extreme. A few miles further distant, the banks were lined with low shrubbery and a few trees, while still higher the banks were lower and the river valley spread out into magnificent meadows and low upland, skirted with fine trees of heavy timber, and stretching miles away before any slope or table-land appeared. Beyond this valley, on the west, are the high hills belonging to the coast range, while far away in the opposite direction loomed the distant, snow-capped peaks of the Sierra Nevada, limiting the view.

Between the opposite towns of Benicia and Martinez, near the mouth of the river, and Sacramento City, there are no settlements, except a few already deserted, an occasional "ranch," or farm house, and a few huts of the wood-cutters. The whole distance from San Francisco to this place is one hundred and twenty-five miles, only a small matter in this "state of magnificent distances."

As we approached the city, the country

grew even more attractive, being higher and more diversified. The river reminded me of the Upper Mississippi, near St. Paul's, although the banks are hardly of sufficient hight to be called *bluffs*. The situation is more inviting, at least I fancied I could see this in the demeanor of the heterogeneous crowd of several steamers that discharged their living freight about the same time. Many of them seemed to step on shore with a sort of satisfied air, as if they owned the land; with something of the pride of proprietorship in the air of independence with which they sallied up the streets to obtain breakfast before leaving for the mines. We landed about sunrise, with the intention of making the tour of the city before breakfast, but after wandering a mile or two, found it not to be in exact accordance with the clamorous voice of the physical man. The city is laid out on a level plain, with wide, straight streets, at right angles, lettered alphabetically one way, and numbered ordinarily the other, making it very convenient for finding strange places. The streets are already laid out to distances almost incredible for so young a city, and can be extended, if necessary, many miles each way, over the level ground of the vast natural park which lies around its site at the confluence of the Sacramento River and the American Fork. There are not wanting men who imagine themselves endowed with prophetic vision, who are forward in predicting that Sacramento will soon be the second city in California, and one of the handsomest in the United States — predictions that seem quite probable, considering the extreme beauty of its locality, the judicious plan upon which it has been commenced, and its great commercial advantages as the chief depot for the mining districts. It seems to me a place of much less show and excitement; society resting upon a more permanent basis than in San Francisco. The people seem more like fixed inhabitants of an old city, having established churches, schools, markets, and places of amusement. I am surprised to find no small number of enterprising young men, emigrants from my own native town, settled in or near the city, doing a flourishing business, or engaged in the grand, primeval art of agriculture. I have also had a pleasing surprise in meeting Mrs. Haynes, my Australian friend, who came on before me, and is now settled and happy at home in Sacramento, fully prepared to appreciate the comparative comforts and luxuries of this adopted home, after the hardships and privations of life in Australia.

29th. — After a few days of enjoyment peculiar to Sacramento, we were ready for a pedestrian excursion to French Creek, thence across the Sierra Nevada to Gold Canon in Carson Valley, the last named and furthest point being nearly four hundred miles from San Francisco. On the second day, at evening, we reached Captain Pike's own homestead, a ranch in the neighborhood of French Creek, which is a branch of the American Fork of Sacramento River, and about fifty miles from the city of the same name. The captain found his tenants still occupying his house and farm, but was a good deal chagrined at finding much of his good, arable land turned upside down; disfigured with holes and ditches by the miners. Proprietorship is no defense in California against this class of men. Where there is gold, a mining claim is paramount to every other, and each man may stake out and work his twenty feet square, if it destroys growing crops, orchards, or undermines the very hearthstone at your feet; — at least, he *will*, and it makes very little difference whether he may. Stopping here a little time, we went up and down the creek, with an eye to the "yellow" discoveries, but found little to encourage us, although we usually obtained our twelve and a half cents per pan, which is generally reckoned the minimum rate at which working is profitable. Here we formed an acquaintance with a young man, who owned a horse, and upon learning our intention of pursuing the journey further, he proposed to join us — an offer which we were glad to accept, as thus our packs might be transported and our progress much facilitated. Our route lay up the valley of French Creek, where the scenery was interesting and beautiful, beside being much more cultivated than we expected. We saw nice farms, large, substantial-looking farm houses, fields frequently of many acres in extent, and fertile gardens here and there between groves of oak or pine. As we passed onward up the valley, the cultivated fields, the gently sloping hills, with their groves of oak, and occasional patches of manzanita or hazel shrubbery, gradually disappeared. Our path was constantly ascending from the time we left Sacramento. The mountains of the Sierra were directly before us, and with every mile the deep canons; dark and rugged ravines grew more numerous, and all the scenery assumed more of the wild and picturesque beauty which is so characteristic of the country. Nevertheless, along the banks of the many small and rapid streams of pure water which here flow down from the mountains, excellent situations for towns and villages are abundant. The narrow valleys and mountain slopes are rich both in vegetable and mineral productions; and the few ranches scattered about here and there have already fully proved the unsurpassed productiveness of the soil, and its fitness for agriculture. If nature has any thing to do with bodily and mental development, these mountain sides may, at no distant day, be peopled with a numerous and mighty race. Some few miles from our starting place, we came out upon Spanish Flat, a secluded, level valley, hemmed in on all sides by lofty mountains, except where its natural drainage flowed out through a narrow gorge, forming the head waters of French Creek.

This isolated and beautiful spot takes its name from a small number of old Spanish families, who have occupied it for many years, living peacefully and contentedly in their pastoral simplicity and wealth. Their descendants would have remained upon the soil in like manner, had not the gold-hunting excitement, with its reckless adventurers, forced a way into this distant retreat. Now the Spaniards have joined the invaders in digging and trading; the banks of their pleasant little forest stream are torn up and dug down, and its channel turned into a new bed; most of the trees and shrubbery have been cut down; houses and stores have been erected upon the mountain sides; a busy thoroughfare winds onward into the mountains, through narrow passes and steep cliffs; and the white tents of the miners, under

PATRIARCH, CALIFORNIA.

oaks and pines, dot all the neighborhood. I have found much pleasure in wandering alone about these forests and mountains, more in delighting myself with the wild grandeur of the scenery than in canvassing for gold, which was my ostensible errand.

I have strolled up and down the place, peering into every canon and valley, finding every where the marks of those who had made unsuccessful experiments and passed onward. Several times I have come upon secret places completely hidden among the mountains, that were occupied by two or three miners, and sometimes by a single, solitary man. These places are technically styled " sly diggings," and their locality is concealed with extreme care by their occupants, who hold them for years together, patiently working from one end to the other, and venturing out for supplies only by night, or by circuitous and concealed routes, for fear others might discover their hiding place, and share their good fortune. Some of these I judged to be making four or five dollars a day. Their professed object is to remain till they have accumulated a " certain pile."

But in all probability some of them will find their graves in these remote regions.

Mud Springs, a little further on, is a large mining town of perhaps twenty-five hundred souls, near to which many thousands of miners are at work, scattered for miles in all directions at the shallow diggings. There is a fair prospect of employment in these mines for a number of years, and it operates as an inducement to the erection of substantial buildings and to general improvement. Most of the inhabitants seem to have made their money moderately, and are quietly and permanently settled, with their families. There are one or two fine churches, and several good school houses; the latter being erected usually by the young men of the vicinity—partly from the disinterested motive of doing good to those who have families, and partly from the desire of having a place for singing schools, evening meetings, political assemblies, or any gathering or occasion of interest which might tend to vary the monotony of the miner's life.

At several points upon our route we had noticed, perched upon the top of some specially

SCHOOL-HOUSE CHURCHES. 283

prominent hill, like the Temple of Science in the frontispiece of Webster's spelling-book, one of these old-fashioned school houses. On one occasion our attention was arrested by a shouting from one of these hills, and looking up, we saw twenty or thirty boys and girls rushing from their prison, in such a tumult of noisy glee, that our momentary impression was, that something extraordinary had happened. The next moment assured us it was *noon*, and we passed on, full of the recollections of youth, and the glorious liberty of school-boy days.

Throughout a great part of the mining country the school houses are the only churches. In them the itinerant preachers, from one and another denomination, fulfil an occasional appointment, preaching to closely-attentive and keenly-appreciative audiences, though not vast in numbers or magnificent in dress. The young men, who usually form the congregation, have nothing but their mining apparel; but they are scrupulously clean. No custom on earth is more rigorously observed than the sailor's and miner's weekly ablutions and clean shirt, even if the wearer has had to wash it himself, and go without any until it was dry. Thus cleansed and clad, the miner feels at once good-natured and independent, and prepared to give a preacher a cordial and respectful welcome, beside paying him bountifully for his labor. These occasional ministrations are enjoyed with the double zest of home associations refreshed, and monotonous drudgery relieved, over and above the pleasure coming from their sympathy in the solemn services, as Christian men.

Two miles beyond Mud Springs is Diamond Springs — a town of similar character and somewhat larger size. Between the two places there exists a rivalry and jealousy of considerable bitterness and activity, made evident to us even in our transient stay, by sneering and depreciating remarks in each at the expense of the other. The result of our observations in this part of our route is, that the miners are a jovial and happy class, living carelessly and at their ease, although at times they know something of hard labor.

The roads here are rough and rather difficult, but pass through a portion of country thick set with lovely mountain scenery. Our path is beset with snakes, which are extremely numerous in California. We sometimes see a dozen rattlesnakes in the course of a day, beside a plenty of a species of adder with a horn in their tail, that are said to sting instead of bite; also a thick-bodied, large-headed snake, here ridiculously called "bulbuls." These, however, seem to be harmless, and we have accustomed ourselves to them. From these springs we proceeded in a straightforward direction, and camped the same night under some tall red-wood pines, the beginning of the celebrated forests of mammoth trees, that stretch through El Dorado and Calaveras counties. Close at hand was a spring of clear water, and abundance of good grass for our invaluable, silent partner — the old gray horse. The next day we journeyed in the shade of these gigantic trees. The day was exceedingly fine, and the mountain scenery magnificent and ever-varying, but the trees absorbed our whole attention. We were prepared to see a few of these leviathan cedars, but to travel miles through forests of them was a perfect wonder and surprise to us.

We had traveled through many forests before, and seen much that was impressive, and even indescribable; but a grove of their trees, though of uncommon size, placed by these monsters, would be like shrubs and bushes in comparison; even their topmost boughs would not reach half way to the lowest branches of these.

These vast and silent forms oppressed and awed us, and we walked on in their broad shadows in reverential silence. It was as if we were transplanted into another world, and another language than ours was necessary to describe the place or its impressions. The trunk of one by which we sat down to rest ourselves was quite smooth and free from limbs, knots, or blemishes of any kind. It rose in one fair, gigantic column, about two hundred feet, and from that hight its enormous cone-shaped head towered away aloft until it seemed to reach the clouds. Such descriptions — in fact, any description — must fail entirely of giving any idea of the truth. It may serve a somewhat better purpose in assisting the imagination to remind the reader that no church spire in the United States would nearly equal these trees in hight—that there are very few whose "weather-cock" would even reach the lowest branches.

One night we spent in "Sly Park," another of the characteristic secret valleys of this region, far beyond any human habitation, surrounded by lofty mountains, seemingly without an opening. The level space within, and the slopes around, were carpeted with bright, wild flowers, of nature's own planting, while here and there stood a group or single tree of the famous red-wood; and at their feet a limpid stream of pure, cold, mountain water. As we relieved our weary horse of his burden, and prepared our meal with the keen appetites of wandering men, the solitude seemed almost sacred, and thought went back to the days of primeval innocence, when earth was arrayed in its early brightness and glory, uncursed by sin, giving neither signs nor sounds of woe. Such reflections were broken, however, by the consideration of necessary precautions against the wild beasts that swarm throughout the California mountains; and, kindling a large fire against the huge dry trunk of a fallen cedar, and another a few rods distant, we laid ourselves down in the space between, lulled to sleep by the low music of the wind through the tops of the trees, and the distant howling of the wild denizens of the forest.

We woke early, refreshed and invigorated by our "siesta" in the pure, mountain air, and by sunrise were pursuing our journey through this valley, which is probably the finest natural park in the world; being very extensive, including within its circuit of many miles a complete system of gentle hills and valleys of its own. These vales are broad and open, of easy slant, and covered with flowers, one variety standing in a bed by itself, and another in like manner further on. Except the towering cedars, there are scarcely any trees, and the view of these kings of the wood is perfect, there being no obstruction from undergrowth or shrubbery. It is almost impossible to escape a humiliating and painful impression of our own utter insignificance in the presence of these ancient giants, by whose side the chestnut of Mount Etna, the cypress of Lombardy, and the great Baobab of Teneriffe are infants in age; and even the ruins of the monuments of the elder races of men are but youthful. It is even affirmed by some that the largest of them have stood for a period dating further back than the creation of man. Sometimes we would meet a group of these trees standing like a family — the tall and graceful form of the parent surrounded by a cluster of half a dozen children growing up symmetrically around her; and again would appear a little dell formed by three or four flowery slopes, and occupied by one solitary and majestic tree. We have met some fallen ruins, that have either been uprooted by mighty tempests or destroyed by fires, probably built by the Indians, who take great delight in this secluded valley. We have met none of them thus far, they being shy and unfriendly mountain tribes of Pah-Utahs and Wah-satch, (usually called Waw-shaws.) The only Indians in the lower country are the few and scattered families of the filthy and unsightly "Diggers," who seem to me even below the Australian natives in intelligence and ability. That they are not remarkable for either high spirit or intelligence is manifest from the fact, that a certain Missourian emigrant, settled in the valley of the Sacramento, actually enslaved quite a number of them; not, indeed, subjecting them to the rough field-hand discipline and severe labor of the plantation, but giving them "quarters" around his mansion, requiring their services, with no reward but some scanty stipend in such manner as he chose. But this probably was far superior to their native, squalid filth, grub-eating, root-digging bill of fare.

The Sierra Nevada ranges, north and south, form the boundary line, in this region, between California and Utah. Upon its eastern side, and separated from us by its whole width, is Carson Valley, extending along under the Sierra a hundred miles or more.

The great emigrant road across the plains comes in at the northern, widest and lowest end of this valley, proceeds south to its extremity among the mountains, and then turning westward, leads over the Sierra into California. Not far from the point where this road comes in from the desert, a trail called the "Johnson Cut-off" turns west, crosses the mountain, and reaches the valley of the Sacramento by a route shorter than the main road, but more difficult. From this there diverges a still more obscure and difficult path, called the Georgetown Trail, which our desire for adventure, and determination to realize the whole of mountain experience, inclined us to follow. As we ascended higher, the scenery grew wild and grand at every step, with steep and rugged mountain slopes—fantastic and endlessly varied forms of crag and pinnacle, interspersed with a growth of trees so thick and strong we wondered they could find room and nutriment. Vestiges of the hardships of a former company, who traveled in this difficult place, are still observed, consisting of ax-marks and branches hewn off at a hight of about forty feet from the ground in some large trees. The condition of these was described to us by a judge in El Dorado, himself one of the company.

The party, numbering nearly a hundred persons, had come across the plain in the season of 1849, rather late, but still in time to cross the Sierra before the fall of the deep, impassable snows in any ordinary season. The snow suddenly set in, however, with uncommon severity, just before they reached Carson Valley. Supposing it would not impede their march, and beside, being unprepared to winter in the valley, if it had been thought necessary, they proceeded, taking the Johnson Cut-off to save time. They found the trail nearly impassable, and a succession of fearful storms continued to assail them on their way. By dint of almost superhuman effort, and after several days of dreadful suffering, they succeeded in crossing the crest of the Sierra, but were yet involved in the labyrinth of ravines and precipices in its upper western portion, when another storm of snow put an end to their march. Here they burrowed holes for lodging, and remained for weeks, helpless and starving, until forty of their number were dead. At this juncture the living gathered strength even from desperation, and succeeded in breaking through to the settlements, and rallying an expedition to rescue the ghastly remainder. The marks of the ax in various trees were made in cutting their fire-wood, creeping about upon the snow.

Our circuitous path led here and there over a saddle-like notch between a tree and the steep hill side; sometimes along a sharp, narrow crest of rock, forming a kind of table to some loftier mass, and again along the face of smooth, bare slopes of granite. Often it was marked only by faintly worn footsteps in the rock; sometimes it was deep with slippery stone dust, while we could hear, faintly, the roaring of the mountain torrent, rushing thousands of feet beneath us, where it was hidden in the dense shrubbery that bordered the dark and narrow chasm. For long distances together it would have been an utter impossibility for another beast to have passed ours. Necessity compelled us to keep a constant watch over each step of our own, for the slightest stumble, or even a dizzy or doubtful movement, would have consigned us to certain destruction. We speculated much as to what could have induced any human being to attempt such a route; much. more to undertake the first passage over it with a laden beast. It must undoubtedly have been traversed by the wild animals of the forest at first; then, perhaps, by observant and agile Indians; by venturesome, athletic, and light-armed mountain men; and last of all, by foolish, reckless Yankees, like ourselves. After much difficulty we landed upon a wild spot directly upon the breast of the mountain, where we could see the highest peak towering above our heads, partly hidden by the fleecy clouds that went floating past it. I proposed to my companions to ascend the peak, which we did, with much less difficulty than we had anticipated, over boulders, ledges, and shelving rocks, till we stood upon an eminence nearly twenty thousand feet high, commanding an almost boundless view of valleys, mountains, forests, lakes, and streams, with a perpendicular descent on one side of several thousand feet. It required strong and steady nerves to look down, or even to stand upon the place.

After descending from the mountain, we discovered some small ponds and hot springs of alkaline water, apparently proceeding from sources within a high mountain of volcanic formation in the vicinity, whose substance, upon examination, clearly seemed a very hard species of lava. By way of experiment, I plunged my hand into one of these springs, and found, as a reward of my scientific zeal, the burning of my fingers and ridicule of my companions.

Scarcely is there a stronger principle in the mind of man than *curiosity*. For this he will endure the burning heat of equatorial regions, brave the rigors of the polar seas, and traverse the wildest land in uninhabited parts, and that in a most uncomfortable manner, with a little commingling of pride, perhaps, that he may have the satisfaction of proclaiming to others the fact of having placed his foot on soil that mortal man beside had never trod. Such tireless energy enlisted in moral reforms, and how soon this world would "bloom as the rose."

CHAPTER XIV.

MORMON REFUGEES. — VISIT ./ GOLD CANON. — EXPERIENCE AMONG THE MO' \INS. — NIGHT IN THE HERMIT'S CAVE. — RETURN TO FRENCH CREEK.

OUR wild, rugged, and winding path, that led us to the Mormon trading post, was not an unapt emblem of the dangerous, deceitful, and wily stratagems of this deluded people. We found a large emigrant train from Salt Lake City — about a hundred large, covered wagons, with an average of five yoke of cattle to each. They had halted for a day's rest on their way to California, this being the first spot this side the Desert where they could obtain supplies of grass and water. Many of them were Mormons, who had forsaken their earthly Canaan, tired, disgusted, and robbed of all their worldly possessions; having managed to escape in company with a Western emigrant train, thankful to get away alive.

Were they to return to the land they had left, they would doubtless be murdered, for the chief axiom of their paradisiac polity is, that "dead men tell no tales."

We heard from the lips of these refugees many sickening details of their Mormon experience. Some of them had repeatedly endeavored to escape from the dominions of their tyrannical rulers, but without success, for the dissatisfied are closely watched, and not permitted to leave the premises at all. Making due allowance for exaggeration, arising from excitement and anger, these stories, which fully agreed in all general respects, indicated a state of things forbidding and terrible in the extreme, in their community, especially in regard to the abject mental servitude which they were obliged to render while they remained. How human beings can be made to believe the absurd articles of the Mormon creed, and to submit to the rule of such miserable, unprincipled leaders, it passes my understanding to conceive. These poor fellows seemed to contemplate with peculiar satisfaction the prospect of speedily entering a land of peace and plenty, where they could have the right of securing to themselves quiet and pleasant homes, to be enjoyed without the fear of being molested by a brutal tyrant.

30th. — After our wearisome march, we are glad to rest a little at the station. It is now the last of June, and the gardens about here are just beginning to look well. Corn and potatoes are just breaking through the ground, and wheat and other grain are about a foot high. The seasons in this valley are so changeable, that no dependence can be placed upon having a full crop of any kind. In general, however, a sufficient quantity of grain and vegetables are raised to supply the wants of the few scattered traders who alone inhabit the valley, beside having a small surplus to sell to emigrants. The water is miserable throughout the valley, with the exception of one or two small streams, that flow down from the mountains; and even these grow warm and alkaline before they proceed far from the heated alkaline sands through which they pass. During the whole time we were on the main emigrant trail, we were never out of sight of dead cattle, poisoned by the water, which has no very strong taste, and which they drink as eagerly as any other.

Beside the creature comforts of grass and water, we have found company in two hard-looking young men, who have been here several days, waiting, as they say, for some train from Horse-town. This latter place, and another similar to it, called Rag-town, are stations eighty or a hundred miles distant from this place, just on the edge of the Desert — rendezvous, both of them, for thieves and all manner of frontier vagabonds, who hang about hoping to find treasures in robbing those who pass their way. The business of our two young friends is doubtless of the same character. The meager willows along the brook not affording us sufficient shelter to camp under, we have been obliged, as often before in Australia, to sleep with the earth for a bed, and the starry heavens for a canopy, and without a fire, notwithstanding the danger of wild beasts' company is still imminent. The weather is excessively hot. To this we are particularly sensitive, so great is the contrast between the deep, sandy roads, open to the burning rays of the sun, and our preceding journey among lofty mountains, frequently under the shade of trees, varied with an occasional snow bank. Yesterday, soon after sunset, it began to grow cold; the wind changed, and instead of blowing from the eastward, across the heated sands of the desert, it came down from the chilly mountain tops, changing the atmosphere suddenly, and rendering us very uncomfortable. Upon rising this morning we found the water frozen in our tin cups — a curious instance of the rapid and extreme variation of temperature, to which the peculiar nature and position of this valley, close beneath the snowy Sierra on one side, and the hot desert on the other, subject it.

Large portions of the northern part of the valley consist of low, marshy tracts, often called "Carson Valley Sink," in which the river of the same name spreads and loses itself. In the summer these dry up, and become, as it were, sheets of white alkali, — soda or nitre, — as hard and smooth as ceiling. The former of these substances is quite extensively used in California for cooking, and various domestic purposes, and serves very well.

We have visited Gold Canon, some miles distant down the river, where we expected to find many miners at work, but were disappointed in learning that nearly all of them had left for California the year before, water having failed them. About fifty, of more daring spirit than the rest, remained, but were finally frozen in and compelled to stay through the winter. They established themselves in houses of slabs, procured a quantity of fuel, and made themselves as comfortable as possible without any communication across the mountains; early in the spring recommenced digging, and had only recently left for California, at the commencement of the present dry season. Only two or three were left; one an aged man, gleaning about on old claims, scarcely making more than a living, and ready to leave at any time. This canon is a narrow ravine, fifteen or twenty miles in length, stretching up westward from Carson Valley, among the lower hills that skirt the range. No canvassing had been done further up than three miles, for fear of the Wahsatch or Wau-shaw Indians, and we dared venture a little further ourselves. It is a strange rift, often not more than twenty yards wide at the bottom, and frequently overhung on both sides with projecting masses of lava, in many curious forms, apparently thus congealed while in motion from some volcanic crater. In the distance these black, bulging masses appeared like solidified thunder clouds, on the point of closing over the chasm. Of such extreme hardness is the rock, we had great difficulty in breaking off a few of the small cubes, into which its substance seems to have crystallized.

I have made some excursions, in company with a young German, with whom I have become acquainted, who has been at work in the mines — a smart, active fellow, formerly employed in the adventurous business of carrying the United States' mail through the enemy's country during the Mexican war. In one instance, we met some traders who gave us such a desperate account of the place we intended to visit, and of the wretches who gathered there, we concluded it was best to abandon the undertaking and return. In a small hollow, out of sight except on very near approach, we found some deserted Indian huts, though having the appearance of being occupied until quite recently. We also discovered a solitary Yankee established in a little "shanty," near the emigrant trail, where he was dispensing manna in the wilderness from a stand, in the shape of ginger cakes, small beer, and sarsaparilla. Business in his line, however, seems not very brisk, and he appeared anxious to sell out.

A young man employed as clerk at a trading post, near us, has shown me quite a quantity of small rubies, procured at a canon sixty miles down the valley. He proposes to unite in an expedition for the purpose of enriching ourselves with more of these sparkling treasures, but as the neighborhood is remote from any white settlement or trading post, and is, moreover, dangerously infested with hostile tribes of Indians, I decline. Beside, I am weary with this desultory exploration. I have seen enough of this barren and inhospitable region, and am disposed, yea, more, *determined*, to go back to Sacramento, let others do as they may.

July 15th. — The use of the pen has been an entirely impracticable thing during the lonely and protracted wanderings in which I have recently been engaged; therefore the leisure that follows must atone for all. When our little company came together among the mountains, to consult upon the matter of returning to civilized society, they promised to be ready on the next day; but feeling disinclined at the appointed time, I expressed my intention of going at any rate; at which a council was called, and an equitable division of our scanty stock of tea and flour made for the emergency.

To this my German friend added a grateful memorial of his friendship in the shape of a piece of ham and a small quantity of tea. Thus supplied, I shook hands with my companions, bade them adieu, and set out to return to Sacramento alone, across the mountains, by the tremendous Georgetown trail — a dangerous trip, not only from the difficulties of the route, but also from the risk of meeting bloodthirsty Indians. But I had seen enough and to spare of Carson Valley, and longed to get back into the embrace of friends, and a less mountainous country, though I had not been without enjoyment of Nature in her most wild and rugged aspects. So, with the perfect recklessness of a genuine mountain man, I hazarded my life to gratify my desire, beside failing somewhat in consistency; for all three of us had avowed most strenuously, a short time before, that no possible consideration could induce us to travel over the road again. In like manner seamen in a storm, or peculiarly rough voyage, often declare nothing will ever tempt them to make another voyage, and then ship again almost the moment they get home. Indeed, I have heard it urged, with some plausibility, that men are very likely to do precisely that which they agree and determine within themselves not to do, and that this is the practical statement of the doctrine of an "*overruling providence.*" Having journeyed twelve miles on my homeward way, I overtook a man traveling in the same direction, evidently of the Anglo-Saxon race, wiry and tall, with brown hair, blue eyes, leathern garments throughout, and a rifle. As we were conversing together on the way, he told me that he had lived two years in the valley, and was now on his way to his place of abode, a few miles from the trail, up a canon in the mountains. He gave me a pressing invitation to spend the night with him, promising that I should lose nothing by leaving the route, as he would take me to it in the morning by a shorter cut. Upon these terms I accepted, and after walking on the road an hour or two, we turned off toward the Sierra, gradually ascending through a rolling country, covered with sage-bush, and swarming with rattlesnakes.

Once, as I stooped to gather some bright-yellow "everlasting," I put my face within six inches of one of these venomous creatures, and only sprang backward at the sound of the rattles in season to save myself from its poisonous fangs. A little further on, as I was earnestly engaged in conversation, my stalwart companion suddenly seized me by the shoulder, and threw me very unceremoniously some distance into the bushes. A thought instantly flashed across my mind that he had enticed me into these wilds to murder me, but I was soon assured it was only a friendly rudeness, to save me from the unfortunate step I was about to take, which would have planted me directly on one of these unwelcome foes. Rattlesnakes, in my opinion, are like many human beings — "*handsome, but hateful.*"

After a little time, we entered a dark and narrow ravine, through which ran a stream of pure ice-water from the top of the mountain, which here towered almost perpendicularly over our heads. The scenery was of a peculiar character, somewhat new to me; the rocks being exceedingly steep and craggy, often forming large, overhanging cliffs and precipices, from whose crevices grew trees and dense shrubbery. The path grew more steep and rugged at every step. For a full half mile we climbed a gigantic natural staircase of shelving rocks, whose foundations were laid in the bottom of the chasm, and so steep and slippery as to require great care and exertion to prevent one's self from falling over backward. At this point the pathway beyond seemed to lose all appearance of regularity, and disappear entirely among the huge rocks and cliffs by the side of the dashing torrent. Still we toiled on, a distance that seemed to me, in my exhausted state, not less than ten miles, but probably not more than two or three.

At last I pleaded for rest, for strength and breath seemed well nigh gone, and further effort seemed vain and useless. He revived my drooping spirits by assuring me it was only a few rods ahead, or rather *overhead*, for, upon looking up, it was evident we could proceed but a little distance, for we were entering a vast cave, whose rocky roof met over us. With one more earnest effort we were at the vestibule of my friend's mansion — a strange and wild abode in truth.

It was walled and roofed with the living rock, while its exterior was gracefully and elaborately adorned with festoons and pendants of thick-trailing plants, growing from every crevice. Within, the smooth stone floor supported natural divans, of the same solid material, which served for store rooms, seats, and bed. In one side was a recess, which served for a fireplace, above which a natural outlet formed a commodious chimney. Close beside the grand arched door-way, a waterfall poured over a cliff, almost hidden by thick foliage, furnishing a perennial fountain of pure, cold water. On either side of the stream, and above us as far as I could see in the shades of the evening, the sharp, craggy rocks projected in such wise as to render it an evident impossibility for man or beast to reach us in any other way but by the path we came. While my host was busy in household matters, I bathed my heated head, neck, and hands in the cool, dashing stream, and sat down outside to indulge in a few moments of repose and romance. The evening was clear and warm, the scene almost one of enchantment for wildness and beauty. As I sat gazing out into the darkness at the dim rocks, I could hear the chirping of crickets, and the voice of a whip-poor-will, mingled with the incessant dash of the roaring waterfall. The moon rose upon me at length with its clear, silvery light, displaying with considerable distinctness the long vista of the rugged gorge through which we had ascended, and further on a portion of the plain below.

All at once I was aroused from my reverie by the howling of wild beasts, seemingly close at hand. "Don't be alarmed," said my host, perceiving my trepidation; "the beasts could not reach us, if they wished to, without going all the way to the plain, and coming up the canon; and they are not likely to take all that trouble for us. Beside, I should not have brought you so far up the mountain just to expose you to wild beasts." Conjecture was busy as to what could have induced him to select such a remote and inaccessible home, so far from any human being, without even a dog for a companion, in absolute solitude, except the invisible animals, whose dismal yells kept up a constant serenade. Something of his history, and the reasons of such conduct, were finally divulged in the course of conversation. He had discovered the cave a year and a half before, while rambling in the mountains, and had occupied it ever since. He was originally from an eastern city, formerly held a good social position, was a man of considerable cultivation, unmistakable marks of which were apparent, and his conversation showed much familiarity with books. He had a few with him, his favorite being "Pope's Essay on Man," and "Zimmerman on Solitude." Trouble and disappointment had driven him from his early home. The tender affections of his heart had been blighted, and he sought relief only in the silent sympathy of nature. A poor antidote, methought, for sorrow, to flee into deserts and caves, existing without human society; and indeed, my host showed that solitude has not its full sweetness without somebody to whom to say that it is sweet. He urged me to remain with him, and share with him his occupations and his castle; but thinking it unfavorable to the development of true character in any sense, I could not think of it. I felt more like saying, with all the earnestness of the captive exile, —

"O Solitude! where are the charms
That sages have seen in thy face?"

Said sages, however, might have seen but few charms, had the sharp eyes of grizzly bears peered at them over rocks, and disturbed them in their slumbers by their howling cries.

We lay down to rest, for the night, upon a bed of buffalo robes, soothed to sleep by the voice of the waterfall, and early next morning the hermit prepared his breakfast of tea, hard bread, and fried ham. The mountain air was clear, cool, and delightfully bracing. As the bright beams of the morning sun shone directly upon and into the long and rocky gorge, lighting up, and reflected from stone, foliage, and dashing water, the dreary place was indeed invested with something of beauty; and I was inclined to consider it a delightful abode, had there only been society, that essential thing to meet the demands of almost every human heart. According to agreement, my new companion directed me on my way, by a path that saved several miles, conducting me safely for a good distance, when he left me, with many regrets and good wishes, to continue my journey alone. At night I camped on the very spot where I with my two associates had spent the night a short time before; kindled my fire on some logs that burned briskly and bright; boiled water for my tea in the same tin cup which I had carried and used daily on the Peytona, the Nautilus, and the Sacusa, in Brazil, Africa, the Isle of France, Australia, and Peru. During the day I had looked forward with no little apprehension to this hour, for I was miles from any human being, in mountain forests, noted for abundance of wild beasts, and haunted in certain portions by hostile Indians. But by the time I had finished my supper, prepared my resting place, replenished my fires, I was quite too weary to allow fear its indulgence, and calmly rolled myself in my blanket, and went instantly to sleep.

Refreshed and invigorated by eight or nine hours of sweet repose, I awoke on the morning of the Sabbath — the sun already high enough to enlighten all the landscape. I sat for a time quietly enjoying the scene; and never have I experienced an hour of more perfect and sacred stillness than then. Not a breeze — not a leaf, was stirring. The mountains, the valley, and the woods were in still repose, save the occasional chirp or twitter of a bird, and the faint gurgle of the brook. All over the vast mountain that towered above me;

the broad, green valley stretching far away below; the groups of trees that crowned the rounded hill on which I sat; the green slopes that curved away to the ravine on either side, and at the end, like the sides of a vast bastion, and even in the pure, motionless air, there seemed to be a pervading spirit of peace and love. I could not have avoided the feeling, even had I wished it, that it was the Sabbath of God that made this lovely Sabbath of nature.

My provisions were scanty, however, and I could not remain. Slowly I resumed my toilsome march among the mountain defiles, sometimes talking and singing to myself as I went, and enjoying the echo of my own voice; for what I repeated in an ordinary tone was often echoed with so much distinctness I involuntarily looked around me to discern some quiet traveler as yet unperceived. Sometimes I sang old songs; sometimes a psalm tune; and often some of the noble chants of the Episcopal church service. This homely music had a curious effect upon my pace, for I repeatedly caught myself walking not so much according to the measure and rhythm of the tune, as to the spirit and life of the words. If I sang a plaintive song or chanted a solemn chorus, I proceeded slowly, and more than once I found myself upon a full run, under the inspiriting influence of some gay and lively ditty. These varied and irregular changes in my speed would doubtless have presented a highly absurd appearance to a spectator knowing nothing of the cause. A habit of self-questioning is very prevalent among mountain men and miners—a very natural one; for having but few companions, they would otherwise speak but little; and the defining power of speech, except to those carefully trained, or unusually gifted with mental clearness, is absolutely essential to connected, satisfactory thinking.

I had so long been accustomed to company in traveling, I began to think my situation dreary in the extreme. The night after the Sabbath found me in the heart of the Sierra Nevada, fenced in with lofty mountains, tipped with snow, while the twinkling stars looked down from the vault of heaven, as if in mournful sympathy with the lonely wanderer. Suddenly a Waw-shaw Indian appeared, with a great fish in his hand, which he had caught in the lake. We exchanged a few words of mountain salutation, and he passed on to his encampment, leaving me with no additional sense of security. The sun went down, the wind began to rise, and soon increased to a gale, sweeping down, in furious, sudden blasts, from the snowy peaks, wailing and whistling, while the trees creaked and murmured. Cold and weary, with only the dim starlight, and ignorant of what perils might be near me, my mind became agitated with uncomfortable fancies. I could see strange shadows moving upon the ground under the trees around me, and hear occasional low cries and sounds, like groans — probably from some beasts in the vicinity.

Welcome indeed was the first coming of dawn; and as soon as I could distinguish the trail I was again on my way. Knowing that I was to cross a high ridge some five miles distant, I determined to try a shorter path, which I fancied would save me a crooked journey around and over the intervening hills. I wandered over ridges and across canons, through woods and streams, until at the end of two or three miles I was entirely bewildered by the endless changes of the scenery, and had quite lost my way. I turned about, and very humbly sought my way to the spot from whence I had diverged, but not without much perplexity. This hour or two of anxiety, while my route was doubtful, afforded me more of mental torture than I had experienced for a long time before. It taught me a lesson, and one that I might have learned in Australia — that it is exceedingly unsafe, especially for one that is alone, to leave the route selected by the combined judgment of preceding travelers, for the sake of any presumed short path or other conveniences. Great was my delight at reaching Diamond Springs, where I could hear the sound of familiar voices. I found them celebrating a public anniversary; the place alive, as it were, with preparations for the gay and joyful occasion. I only delayed to call upon a few friends, and passed on to French Creek, where I have established myself at the ranch of Captain Pike, where I purpose to spend some days in gold-hunting in the vicinity.

Hard labor, however, is out of the question; for I am more desirous of quiet rest than great pecuniary gain. Here, in a secluded canon, quite alone, I shall have opportunity for much solitary meditation, beside the prospect of making about five dollars a week, free of expense. The proportion of those who really earn any large amount is quite as small in California as in Australia.

If any one would have a sample of gold digging, no more satisfactory experiment could be made than to take some street where the ground is very hard, dig a drain in it, perhaps six feet in depth, three in width, and of any desirable length. While working at the lower foot of this, all the earth, more especially the lumps and harder pieces, should be rubbed to fine powder between the hands, closely inspected, and then thrown away. Such is the actual experience of the miners, and that with continual disappointment and "hope deferred."

Thus looking at these things, the admonition of the wise man to search for "wisdom" as for hid treasures, becomes invested with a tenfold deeper meaning to one at all inclined to spiritualize ordinary things and events.

CHAPTER XV.

RESIDENCE AT SAN FRANCISCO. — LIFE ON STEAMER CORTES. — MISSIONARY TOUR. — SCHOOL TEACHING. — CAMP MEETING.

So infrequent were my journalizing entries during a great portion of my life in California, by reason of busy occupation or busy wandering, I propose to give in the present chapter a review of the whole, or mainly, with incidents connected thereto, as I contemplated them December, 1855, a short time before leaving for New England.

After returning from the mountains, and spending some time at French Creek, I took up my residence at San Francisco for two months, not engaged in any fixed occupation, but rendered somewhat uneasy by idly living in one place so long. In California, particularly, "labor is honorable;" and professing a hearty sympathy with this healthy tone of public opinion, I at length established myself in business, by gathering quite a number of subscribers to various weekly and monthly periodicals, purchasing at a fair rate from importers by wholesale, and delivering at retail prices immediately upon their arrival. During this time I gained many pleasant and profitable acquaintances, among whom was a gentleman in the "pop-corn" business, who was quite "an institution" in the city, receiving a net profit of something like ten dollars a day by his operations. He was a shrewd Massachusetts Yankee, had fully matured his plans before coming out, and was ready for action on his arrival. His corn was shipped to him from New England, around the Horn; he parched it himself at night, and with not less than eighty or a hundred quarts, modestly promenaded the streets with an enormous basket on each arm, waiting on chance or regular customers in a very quiet way, in no wise detracting from his dignity. Indeed, he filled the office just as a dignified republican ought to fill any office, being a valuable member of society, and at the same time consulted his own best interests.

Having laid up some money, and being able to command a little credit and influence, my views began somewhat to enlarge, and I conceived a plan for establishing a bookstore, in company with a young man of my acquaintance. Ere the thing was decided in the mind of my proposed partner, another opportunity presented itself of employment in another direction. Another acquaintance, who had been storekeeper on the steamship Cortes, running between San Francisco and San Juan del Sur, on the Nicaragua route, was about to give up his place, and offered to aid me in securing the position if I wished. Promptitude is the first of practical virtues, especially in California; and acting on this, the bookstore scheme was dropped, the kind offer of my friend accepted, and I was speedily installed in my new post, once more floating on salt water.

The position of storekeeper on one of these large ocean steamers is one of no small responsibility and influence. The steamer itself, with its multitude of passengers, constitutes a kind of floating city, with great interests and great revenues. We were accustomed to carry about three hundred first-cabin passengers, at three hundred dollars each, making ninety thousand dollars; and five hundred in the second cabin, at one hundred and fifty dollars; which, together with what was realized from freight, often amounted to the handsome sum of one hundred and eighty-five thousand dollars the single trip. Including passengers, officers, and crew, the whole number of souls on board was usually about a thousand; and by virtue of my office, I was in charge of all the provisions and groceries for this large number, which it was my duty to serve out daily, according to the written demands made upon me by the steward. I found myself at once a universal favorite among the ship's company, treated by all (except, of course, the superior officers) with a degree of attention which I was scarcely conscious of deserving, and which I could scarcely account for, until I learned that my position enabled me, even without violating any obligation, to show many trifling favors, in matters of gastronomy. Then the reason of the flattering regard was clear; and had I chosen to be a little less virtuous, it is difficult to tell what the limits of my influence might have been. It was on board this ship I first knew the unfortunate steamship Yankee Blade. She lay upon the other side of the dock we occupied, and left the city at the same time with us. She was an immense vessel, crowded beyond all description. I gazed in perfect astonishment at the mass of human beings that crowded her every part as she glided away from the wharf into the bay. She could not have had less than fifteen hundred souls on board, more than a thousand of whom were lost this same trip, in the fearful wreck it experienced. Suspicions of foul play were in the minds of many, for she carried an immense treasure beside what was in the hands of the passengers, and ran upon the beach in a clear night, in calm weather, in a manner that has always remained a mystery.

During the second voyage in the steamer Cortes, I made an excursion to the Pearl Islands, which are scarcely more than a group of low rocks and reefs in the sea, the largest only being inhabited, and that by a sort of old patriarch, and fifteen or twenty Indians, who have to bring their water from the main land, and who live by fishing. Here we obtained about twenty varieties of pearl oysters, cypreæ, &c., some quite rare and valuable. We gathered many that yet contained the living inhabitants, quaintly formed molluscs, fantastically mottled, striped and speckled with bright colors, giving a very different impression of the natural history of the class from that derived only from the study of the dry shell. My life on shipboard, during these two voyages, was not marked with any incidents of special interest. The duties of my occupation kept me closely confined to the store room most of the time, and leisure at command was employed in assisting the purser in writing. The confinement in such hot, oppressive atmosphere telling sensibly upon my health, I availed myself of the first suitable occasion to resign, and went on shore again. The mate left at the same time, purchased a vessel, and made a proposition which I conditionally accepted, to accompany him as a sort of supercargo in a trading voyage to China and the seas adjacent; but this, it seems, was not "to be my destined end and way." While determining and securing the necessary outfit, I fell in with Rev. Mr. Richardson, who was about making a tour of exploration, in behalf of a missionary body, through Petaluma and Santa Rosa valleys and the country thereabout. I at first declined his invitation to join him in this excursion, on account of sailing for China; but finding that I could return in season, I concluded to accompany him, and we took the steamer together for Petaluma. We crossed the bay, and entered the creek, to which a spur of the coast range extends, skirting its valley with a margin of low, conical hills; some rugged and wild in outline, and others rounded and smooth; some thickly wooded with oak and mansanita bushes, and others quite bare, except for a thick coat of "wild oats," which were just springing up fresh and green, it being the growing month of January. The creek is the most crooked stream I have ever navigated, winding about in the most extravagant manner, as if anxious to detain all comers as long as possible. Upon reaching the town, we found it to be a scattered collection, mostly of wooden houses. We proceeded to the tavern, where, in looking over some pictures, I was startled to behold the face of a friend, whose location in the wide world I had not known for years, but who, my hostess informed me, was not more than ten rods distant — the principal of a flourishing school of one hundred and fifty students. We immediately repaired to his school house — a roomy and convenient building, well fitted, and furnished with modern desks, maps, globes, and other apparatus, giving to it a character and solidity that quite surprised and pleased us, and at once produced favorable impressions of the progress of this rural district in education and general intelligence.

From this place we proceeded to Petaluma Flat, or rather across it, to the dwelling of "Father Guernsey," which we found with little difficulty, as every one knew the home of the venerable man. We found him working at his trade of chair making, and understood that both himself and chairs were known in the vicinity, there being no other one of the profession in the place, and none other who, like him, devotes all the time and strength which he can spare from business to the spiritual wants of the population.

Upon learning our errand, he received us with cordial hospitality, and laying aside his tools, proceeded to give Mr. R. much and judicious information relative to the purpose of his trip.

He was a man of commanding presence, with fine head and features, full of kindness and intelligence; had resided in the place three years, and was able to speak of the moral and intellectual condition of the people with some degree of accuracy. After spending a social hour with him at his table, he spoke of an appointment to hold a prayer meeting, and invited us to accompany him thither, adding, in a rather significant way, that the Home Missionary Society had sent out a man to help him, and that he would conduct the exercises of the hour. The place of assembly was a log school house, a mile or two away on the Petaluma side of the creek. The gathered worshipers were thirty or forty plain men and women, some of them rough emigrants, mostly from the Western States, yet of warm hearts, and sincere, though blunt, in speaking of things divine as well as temporal. They seemed to have come together for earnest and affectionate communion with each other, and to pour out their hearts unitedly before God.

The missionary entered, — a spruce, dignified young graduate from an eastern theological seminary, — clad in garments of spotless black. There were a few moments of silence, when the young brother rose and offered a short but earnest prayer, after which he read a hymn, which was sung by the little company. A pause of full ten minutes ensued, in no wise disturbing the gravity or dignity of the young divine, and then the benediction was pronounced, and the assembly was dismissed. There was something so irresistibly comic in the utter helplessness and complete frustration of the divine, that few faces were without a smile, giving rise to the apprehension that many had more of fun in their hearts than religious consolation as the effect of the meeting.

I realized at once the difference, not between the religions, but the religious exercises of the eastern seminary and the western heart. This young clergyman would doubtless have done well at home, with a few active Christian men to sustain him, where every thing is done by a kind of rule; but here, where there is no particular rule, where all denominations are fused together, and where very little is said, or can be said, except from the overflowings of rude but honest hearts, the poor man was as helpless with his theology and his ways, as if he had come to swim in the ocean with fetters on.

Next morning, Mr. R. and myself made a little excursion some twenty miles up the country, in the direction of Santa Rosa, stopping at almost every house in the prosecution of our inquiries. Nearly all the inhabitants are Pikes, or from the region adjacent to that famous county of Missouri which is commonly called "the State of Pike," and which has contributed a very large and distinctly marked element to the population of California.

We found a very few Bibles, and scarcely

any books, or printed matter of any kind, except a portion of the miserable "yellow-covered literature" which has had so immense a sale in this state as well as most others. In spite of ignorance and uncultivation, however, there was a hearty, overflowing hospitality and good feeling about the people that really delighted us. Every one was glad to see us, pleased at our errand, and as anxious as any apostle could have desired for the establishment of schools and churches in the land.

Thus exploring and inquiring, we reached Santa Rosa, a thriving place, and the county seat, situated in the midst of a vast natural park not quite as large as Petaluma. Here I left Mr. Richardson, in order to return, but not without strong and repeated solicitations that I would abandon my intention of foreign travel, and engage in teaching school in the valleys of Sonoma county. My own inclinations were at once in favor of so doing, for I felt myself exceedingly charmed with the lovely landscape, the perfect climate and rich soil of the region, as well as the free and open-hearted character of the people. Not wishing to be hasty, however, I avoided giving any answer, and returned to Petaluma, where I found my friends anxious for the same thing. Indeed, the eagerness of the Petaluma people, men, women, and speculators, for the growth and improvement of their place, passed all my conceptions, though, doubtless, the ambition of the latter was strongly tinctured with selfishness. The place numbered some five hundred souls, and was still increasing. We were wont to say the town grew with every arrival of the boat. Especially did the crowd at the landing place rejoice if they could discern the face of a woman on deck. For every bonnet they could count, the real-estate proprietors said to themselves, "So many building lots sold at paying prices." I have actually seen tears in the eyes of these earnest watchmen at an unusually large feminine immigration, evidently from pure joy at the prospect of their remunerative sales. "Every tear is a dollar," remarked a friend of mine one day, as he pointed out one of these lachrymose rejoicers.

Having consulted with my friends at San Francisco, and finding their advice to coincide with my own preference, I notified my friend, the captain, of a change of plans; fully determined to cast in my lot among the free-hearted and stirring people of the valley of Petaluma. I took a ranch near the centre, which consisted of a few acres fenced in, a small but comfortable house, of redwood slabs, and "all creation" back of me, to the Pacific Ocean, for a grazing range. A friendly housewife offered to supply me with milk; different farmers allowed me the free use of their horses, and thus I was installed landholder, housekeeper, and citizen of the town of Petaluma. I soon had the pleasure of receiving my sister and her family to my home, which now assumed the more dignified cognomen of "country seat," in connection with, and in distinction from, their city residence. During the whole warm season, it was gladdened by the city people, who took great satisfaction in the clear, country air, and the rude but healthful country regimen.

The chosen location for my school was Vallejo township, not far from my ranch. Father Waugh, the chairman of the committee, was an excellent and much-respected citizen, a pioneer settler of the region, having been obliged to leave Missouri, his native state, on account of anti-slavery sentiments.

The examination was brief, the most difficult question being "Do you keep *loud* or *still* school?" I had not known the distinction, and, after a moment's reflection, answered at hazard, — reasoning, "a priori," that the most quiet school is the best, — that I kept *still* school, *by all means*. The demeanor of the committee assured me I had given the right answer; the certificate was granted, due notice given, and I met my pupils in the school house — a set of hearty, good-natured boys and girls, the majority of them Missourians by birth or parentage. Ignorant of their previous discipline and present attainments, and desirous of gaining some acquaintance with their ways, I simply announced that they might take their books and proceed in the usual manner. It was then I learned the full significance of "loud school." Opening their well-used books, every one, at the full stretch of their voices, began studying their various lessons aloud; some standing, some sitting, others summoning assistance from the further side of the room, and still others leaving the house and coming back at pleasure. One day of such experience was amply sufficient, and the second I proceeded to classify and arrange more according to my mind, and speedily had the satisfaction of seeing my little kingdom upon a footing more consistent with the character of a good school. I succeeded in varying the regular succession of ordinary school exercises, much to the acceptance of the young people, by a singing and spelling school, which was held in the evening, and passed off with great enthusiasm.

All parties expressed entire satisfaction, and I was fain to console myself with this glory, in the loss of wealth which accrued to me by reason of the failure of many of my employers to pay me my dues. They were good friends; unvaryingly kind and hospitable; but they were by nature careless, by habit more so in pecuniary matters; and in this purely agricultural community of new settlers, many of them really had not the money at command. They were ready to turn out whatever they had — one man a lot of hogs; one a quantity of growing trees from his nursery; and another some summer butter; but being quite disinclined to the bartering business, I preferred to let the balance, some hundred and fifty dollars, remain uncollected. The trip I made to the school superintendent's residence, to obtain his authority in enabling me to draw my share of public money, was very characteristic of California life. He lived — nobody knew exactly where — somewhere up in the woods beyond Santa Rosa. I could scarcely afford to wait his uncertain coming; so, obtaining a horse, I started in pursuit of him. Coming within four or five miles of the neighborhood where I expected to find him, my path was interrupted by a broad "slew" of black mud, of uncommonly sticky appearance. It must be tried; and on we went, and in two jumps my gray horse was saddle deep, and still sinking. I grasped the end of the long tether, and by a violent effort, succeeded in throwing myself upon firm ground, on the further side. By sharp discipline then extricated my horse, but in such a condition as to make further riding out of the question. I therefore led him the rest of the way, and toward dusk arrived at the residence of Dr. B. in a woeful plight. Mrs. B. appeared at the door of her slab mansion, holding up her hands in astonishment, and exclaimed, "Here, doctor, go get a hoe and scrape this man before he comes into my house!" Her obedient lord obeyed, and then brought me before a vast fire of logs, in an enormous chimney place, before which I stood, turning round and round, like a turkey dangling by a string to roast, until I was completely dried. With due brushing and a refreshing supper, I was metamorphosed into a new man, spent the evening in pleasant conversation, transacted my business, and next day returned to Petaluma by a different and less muddy route.

During my term of teaching, which occupied some six months, I made many pleasant and valuable acquaintances; was also able to make myself of some service by rendering occasional assistance at the few religious services of the neighborhood, which were the only substitute, in these remote valleys, for the stated Sabbath meetings of older eastern communities. Much the most striking religious solemnity, however, at which I was present, was the yearly camp meeting attended in the woods.

This *institution* is the natural and appropriate outgrowth of the weeds and peculiarities of the western mind. In the Eastern States, where the regularly organized assemblies for worship are sufficient for all, these forest gathings are superfluous, unnatural, and out of place, and by necessary consequence, almost absurd and harmful, being little better than occasion for riot and frivolity.

In the thinly-settled and poor communities of the new Western States, among a people who can but rarely support settled ministers, and whose whole mental and moral nature is of a type, out of all comparison more spontaneous, fervid, and sympathetic than that of their deliberate and cautious brethren at the east, these great gatherings are a true and proper expression of religious sentiment, consistent, and agreeing with the enthusiasm of their political mass meetings, and the thoroughgoing energy of their business enterprise.

Every year, in August, it is usual, in Sonoma county and elsewhere, to hold these general jubilees. Christians of all denominations meet in some open grove, near a stream of water, and remain, according to circumstances, a few days or longer. The worshipers gather sometimes from a circle a hundred miles in diameter, and remain in tents during the continuance of the meeting. Denominational differences are laid aside, and the entire proceedings conducted in the broadest and most harmonious spirit of universal Christianity. At the single meeting I attended, I was astonished at the depth and evident truthfulness of religious feeling which was manifested. It was here I witnessed one of those impressive and extraordinary spectacles sometimes peculiar to these occasions. At the close of a long and fervid season of prayer, exhortation, and singing, came a short pause, which was interrupted by a woman, who stepped in front of the desk. She was crippled and bent by disease, but possessed high and striking features, dark, expressive eyes, and every appearance of strong and elevated character. In a clear, musical voice, and in natural and appropriate words, she narrated to the hushed and startled audience a short story of suffering and sorrow, and described the consolation she had found in religion amid it all; adding, that the only thing remaining for her to ask was, that her only children, a son and a daughter of adult age, then and there present, might share with her in the hopes of Christianity; and she called upon all to join their prayers with hers that this crowning blessing might be granted to a widow, and a woman of many sorrows. Then kneeling at once upon the place, she poured out her soul in a prayer of such passionate fervor, such beseeching earnestness, as melted the hearts of all. It is impossible to describe the emotion visible upon every countenance; but when the two children, in very truth, did issue from the crowd and knelt beside their aged mother, their eyes streaming with tears of repentance and gratitude, mingled together,— when it appeared that the blessing had descended even while they sought it,— there was an almost overwhelming outburst of sympathetic joy. Scarcely a face within the tent, crowded as it was with wandering, toil-hardened, weather-beaten men and women, inured to hardship and suffering, but streamed with tears; indeed, so strong was the tempest of feeling, it was impossible, for some considerable time, for either ministers or hearers to resume the regular order of exercises. It must be a shallow soul — one-sided, ignorant, scant of human instincts, and of just thought, or, at least, wofully hampered with fetters of precedent and habit — that would refuse to recognize the suitableness and power of such gatherings, especially in these new places. Nor is it any argument against them that their more grave and impressive features are occasionally varied by others even of a ludicrous character.

It was during this same meeting I entered one of the tents in the midst of an enthusiastic hymn, which was sung, as usual, by the entire congregation. I took the only vacant seat, which brought me in close proximity to a good old colored woman of large proportions, well known in the vicinity as "Aunt Peggy."

She bore her part in the singing with all the enthusiasm of the African character — shutting her eyes, and rocking to and fro with great quickness of motion. Opening her eyes, she suddenly caught a glimpse of me; and with a face perfectly radiant with joy and true benevolence, she cried out, forgetting every thing except the glories of heaven, and the hopes of reaching them herself, and meeting her friends there, "Bress de Lord, broder Welles, I didn't know you was so near me! We'll go to heaven togeder — won't we?" and therewith threw her arms about my neck in a most fervent embrace. The dismay and staring confusion of certain young ministers who were present, and, like him of Petaluma, fresh from an eastern theological seminary, may be imagined. They sat in silent amazement, unable to speak or sing. They had intended to assist in the exercises of the meeting, but had no power to do it, even in spirit. One of them, meeting me at the close of the evening, whispered cautiously in my ear, "I don't understand this, brother Welles; I never saw any thing of this kind before. I don't know what to make of it. You think it all correct and expedient — do you?" I comforted the good man as well as I could; but nothing short of a thorough putting off of all his preconceived opinions about forms and observances, and an assimilation to these new ways of thinking and acting, can reconcile him to the scenes of a California camp meeting; and such a change is not the work of a day, especially for the graduate of an eastern seminary. In proportion to one's adaptation to circumstances is his power to enjoy a new country, with its customs and manners more or less strange, and his ability to do good. My quota of enjoyment has been realized in this delightful portion of the world. In after years memory will revert to these scenes with peculiar pleasure. I go now to my native land, to the scenes of my early youth, the friends I love; and if life is spared to recount to them the adventures of my recent history, I shall have occasion to say on every hand,—

"Thus far the Lord hath led me on."

CHAPTER XVI.

VOYAGE HOME. — ATTEMPT AT SUICIDE. — NATURAL FEATURES OF CALIFORNIA. — REFLECTIONS UPON MEN AND MANNERS. — SUPERIORITY OF AMERICAN CHARACTER.

My residence in Petaluma might have lasted a lifetime, perhaps, had not a combination of circumstances rendered it seemingly necessary for me to return to New England. My voyage across the Isthmus was without any special interest, unless it was an attempt at suicide which was made as we were entering Panama Bay. It was a young girl, disappointed, and for the time nearly crazed, by not meeting friends whom she had expected on her way. She jumped overboard from the steamer, intending to escape from such a troublesome world by drowning. The sea water, and the tremendous idea of death which came from the sense of its absolute nearness, worked an instantaneous revulsion in her feelings, and she implored them to rescue her. Being floated by means of her dress, the boat of the steamer was sent out, and she was brought on board mortified, and apparently satisfied to live as long as she could. A fair opportunity to see how it would seem would probably prevent a vast majority from prosecuting their suicidal folly.

I reached my native land after about three years of absence, most of it consumed in the wanderings of the desultory circumnavigation, the adventures of which I have related, not with any particular ecstasies of patriotism or joy, but, as in regard to most other human events, with mingled emotions of pain and pleasure. A large portion of my time was spent in California, and therefore impressions of life in this place are more vivid and distinct than those of any other. California is, indeed, a splendid country to live in. Its atmosphere, not only natural, but social and mental, has a strangely invigorating and pleasing effect upon those issuing from the comparatively conventional and humdrum life of the old states at the east.

There is a free, truthful, and sincere activity, strength, and decision, in the society exceedingly attractive to most minds. Both men and women are deeply interested in whatever relates to the welfare and prosperity of the Pacific state. The Vigilance Committee, and various other organizations of the kind outside San Francisco, are to be reckoned not lawless or rebellious, but simply as spontaneous combinations for suppressing wrong and upholding the purity of the republic — such as would be impossible in an eastern state or city, solely for the lack of the requisite union of honesty and vigor in political and moral character.

The broad, clear vigor of mind shown so early in the existence of the state is to be accounted for partly in the natural action of strong and right-minded men, thrown together under circumstances which render them at once independent in courses of individual life, thought, and action; and singularly inter-dependent in all the purposes of action as a united people.

Another cause, perhaps hardly less efficient, is the stimulating power of this region. There is a strange and peculiar exhilaration in the very air of California, which belongs also to the whole vast range of the Pacific basin. Many seem equally content to settle or to roam about the lands or the waters of this enchanted realm.

A story was told me of a wealthy young Scotchman, — a baronet it was said, — who owned a swift and beautiful schooner, and constantly lived in her — the life, as it were, of a proud sea-king. His little craft now and then entered the harbor of San Francisco, or was heard of at Honolulu, or some other distant port, having put in for supplies. At other times he was cruising to and fro, or delaying at his pleasure at some beautiful island harbor, enjoying the delights of sun and air, earth and ocean, in the paradise of the South Pacific — as nearly a perfect life as the world can furnish for physical pleasure.

I have known more than one instance where emigrants from the east have resided for a while in California, grown homesick, and returned only to find themselves, after a short stay, pining still more strongly for the balmy air and magnificent climate, the fruit and flowers they had left, than for the old associations, conveniences, and privileges of their eastern home.

There is no winter except a rainy season, which lasts from October to April, during which frost is unknown. The temperature of the first January of my stay ranged from fifty to seventy degrees; scarcely a day when one might not take a pleasant and healthful walk in the open air.

The climate is without either extreme; being no frost in winter or dog-days in summer. There is always a sea breeze at night along the coast, and an occasional morning fog is dispersed by the sun at about ten o'clock, A. M., in season for a day warm, but not oppressive. The harsh, dry heat, the raw Atlantic fogs, the piercing cold of north-east storms, are unknown. It is doubtless the healthiest country in the world.

Farming and gardening are a wonder to the eastern man, with his long winter, hot and hurrying summer, hard and meager soil, and his severe labor. No stores of winter fodder are needed; there is not one day in the year when he cannot work in the ground. One Bodega potato has been known to suffice two or three men at dinner. Grains of different kinds more than double the Atlantic crops. Fruit is yielded from seed or cuttings a full year sooner than at the east. Fresh vegetables and fruit are in the market at San Francisco every month in the year; and to the whole circle of productions of the Northern States are added many more of almost tropical character. Figs grow and prosper in the open air, and the nutmeg is a native production of one portion of the state. In favorable exposures there is little doubt that a large class of the distinctive tropical fruits could be produced with slight protection, if not actually naturalized.

Petaluma and its neighborhood, where I spent a greater part of my time, is a very paradise for the farmer. Almost the whole of Sonoma county, which is as large as the entire State of Connecticut, lies in a broad and fertile valley of rich meadows and grassy uplands, a hundred and fifty miles in length, and from forty to eighty broad, whose natural riches and capabilities are but little known even in San Francisco. Many of the farmers entered this region ten years since, purchased land of the Spanish proprietors, and entered at once upon the business of cattle raising, killing them chiefly for the hides, at a profit perhaps of two dollars a head. The gold discoveries, and the cities that have consequently grown up around them, have put a stop to these wasteful operations, and many large fortunes have been made by the sale of meat and produce to the mountain miners and city markets. These opportunities for certain and regular profits from agriculture increase every year with the growth of city and country.

With these advantages, and the valuable resources of gold, quicksilver, and other metals and minerals; with a population already numerous and ever increasing, and a territory capable of supporting twenty millions, at the rate of population per square mile of the State of New York; and with the present prospects for moral and intellectual improvement from the educational, benevolent, and religious influences and institutions already established and operating, — it is impossible to limit the splendor of the future for California.

The chief inquiries that have been propounded to me by those to whom I have rehearsed the reminiscences of my travels, are such as these: "What were you driving at? What were you trying to do? What is the result of it all?" In the first place, at the point of departure, I was a discouraged man, unhappy in mind, weak in body, and not without symptoms of pulmonary disease. With a substantially rebuilt constitution, it has given me contentment and an equability of mind altogether above valuation. It is true I can not lay down any plan upon which I proceeded, covering the entire time and space of my travels. I did not go with a settled purpose of obtaining information, nor gold, nor "specimens," nor after any thing else that I could tell, although I returned with more or less of all these. I could boast a collection of shells numbering five thousand or more, and of no small value for scientific purposes; a good, though less extensive collection of minerals, including gold and silver ore, agates, cornelians, bloodstones, pearls, and many miscellaneous curiosities; beside an inexhaustible store of recollections of persons, places, and things; of manners and customs; observations upon human nature, which are continually doing good service by furnishing material for comparison and reflection.

In spite of the lack of any abstract unity of purpose, or any elaborate plan, — even though I can only say that an instinct for wandering carried me along,— I apprehend most men will count these three years as far from misspent. In what other way the fruits of travel can be gained I have yet to learn; and I am further ignorant of any experience so rich and available as sources of knowledge of men and minds. During the latter part of my stay abroad, and since my return home, I have met with some few of the various companions of my wanderings; and the intelligence I have been able to gather respecting the unlucky Peytona may not be uninteresting to those who have followed her through a disastrous, shifting, and "shiftless" voyage. She was condemned and sold at Port Louis, on account of her passengers remaining there; bringing about nine thousand dollars, which gave to each person about fifty dollars to enable them to leave the island. The price was given for the beauty of her model, which was one of the first and best of Donald M'Kay's long line of triumphs in clipper ship building, rather than for any great value in her strained and weather-beaten hulk. She was thoroughly rebuilt, christened again by a name I do not know, and is probably at this moment plying about the Indian Ocean, or China Sea, laden with sugar or opium, swarming with centipedes and scorpions, and manned by rice-eating, inefficient Lascars. What became of the captain, his swearing mate, and mutinous crew, I know not. The fortunes and misfortunes of the hapless company would doubtless be a curious chapter in the history of human affairs, were they known.

Advice which I can give to travelers is of trifling moment, and can of course be applied only to those whose journeyings are similar to my own. Seasickness — that frightful thing, concerning which so many speculate, and which many know by a meaning deeper than speculation — is one of those things to be considered on a long voyage. My belief is, that no precaution whatever can be relied upon; that some persons will never feel it; that some may escape it, by attention to diet before embarking; by being much in the open air, or preserving a horizontal position on board; and that others will have it under any circumstances whatever. Persons of a sanguine and nervous temperament are most subject to it. The resolute maintenance of good temper, cheerful endurance of whatever befalls, and above all, a continual endeavor to be helpful and encouraging to others, are points of cardinal importance to the traveler; for the mind occupied in alleviating the miseries of others is certain to forget its own. By practicing some such hints, with others suggested by wiser travelers, and such as every one's own foresight or experience may dictate, the various difficulties and hardships incident to "second-class" style of traveling, which necessity compelled me to adopt, may be much lightened. Yet, after all, this mode cannot be recommended, if by any possible means it can be avoided, as its influence upon character is far from being desirable. One is thus thrown, usually, among the vulgar and ignorant, where he must absolutely practice a sharp system of self-defending circumspection, and assertion of his own rights, nearly bordering upon selfishness and dishonesty; and very naturally slides into the opinion that whatever wrong doing he is tempted to commit, will remain unknown to the circle of his friends and home neighbors, among whom his reputation chiefly exists. The steady operation of these influences, so dilapidating to the strength and perfection of the moral sense, is hardly ever counteracted, even for a little time, by the society of the good.

The decided tendency of traveling any way, is to develop into a master-passion the innate disposition in the human mind to lead a restless, roving life. Too many of the great army of men who have left the United States within the past few years, have either become irreclaimable wanderers, or returned to their homes discontented, unhappy, aimless and useless. In that large class who are driven away from home, or fancy they are, by domestic or other troubles, we find these effects very naturally intensified. Thus the man who left home a very respectable member of society, with good intentions and habits, a perception of right and wrong, a sense of obligation to God and man, and in the habitual practice of some effort at improvement of mind and soul, often becomes, if nothing worse, improvident, reckless, careless of every thing except the comfort and pleasure of the present day, sinking in every respect far below the dignity of his nature. My own countrymen I invariably found to be superior, in most respects, to those of other countries and nations.

Their most unseemly trait is inquisitiveness, which they gratify without regard to things divine or human, in a manner often insufferably impertinent. Curiosity is no less apparent. This characteristic shone forth with wonderful power during our stay at Bahia, where our fellow-passengers visited every church, handling pictures, images, and every thing within reach. Many a dark stain was left upon white marble statues, gilded picture frames, and other ornamental fixtures, all over the city, to attest the rigid investigation of these peering visitors. When they had seen the building, they applied themselves to the worshipers. I have seen devotees kneeling before an image, praying with the absorbing fervor of a sincere Romanist, apparently unconscious that they were quite surrounded by the curious faces of a dozen strangers, watching to see "how they did it."

Many more were those who wrote or carved their names, with dates or strange devices, in all manner of places — a custom of erecting monuments to one's self, which, however, is no more common among Americans, who have no other way of becoming celebrated, than among cockneys, or any other class of wanderers.

These demonstrations were a cause of wondering disgust to the inhabitants, who will not even mind their own business, if they can help it, much less any body's else. Their quiet, listless ways were a constant surprise to us. Nobody gazed at us in the churches or in the streets. Under circumstances that would have drawn the attention of every eye in a New-England church, we might have entered a Romish cathedral without receiving even a look from the listless or earnest devotees.

Having said this, the worst is said. In all other respects whatever, Americans abroad are beyond measure superior to all other nations in morality, good manners, good nature, good companionship, friendliness, and generosity; this, however, not urged in competition with the remarkable, thorough-going, and almost universal display of the last three qualities among English seamen. In business, shrewdness, energy, tact, invention, and success, they far exceed all others. All improvements at Ballerat in the process of mining had been made by Yankees, and the same may be said in other directions.

One, however, prosecuting any enterprise, is obliged to encounter the whole strength of a bitter and ignorant national dislike, by reason of much prejudice against foreigners, which is more or less strong in all places.

The homely rhymes of the poet will finally

serve to express a yet more comprehensive summary of my experiences: —

> "This world is not so bad a world
> As some would choose to make it;
> But whether good or whether bad,
> Depends on how you take it."

There is good in the world, and about almost every body in the world; and he who looks out keenly and good naturedly, not only for himself, but for others, will be sure to succeed.

He will, in a certain sense, be a friend of "God and Mammon" — two effective allies; for men help him who helps them, and "God helps him who helps himself."